JULY 2012

DEAR VALERI_

MAY THIS BOOK _

ENCOURAGEMENT + INSPIRATI_

AS YOU ENTER THE

BLESSED SEASON + ADVENTURE

OF MOTHERHOOD.

YOU'RE GOING TO MAKE

A WONDERFUL MOTHER!

LOVE,

MIKE

Presented to _____

By _____

Occasion _____

Date _____

# Remembering Mother

When all the children have grown and gone,
Which memories of Mother will linger on?
Will it be the time she dried their tears,
Held them close and calmed their fears?

The way she always found the time
To read their favorite nursery rhyme,
Over and over, time and again,
Until they knew it, beginning to end?

The sleepless nights with an ailing child—
Mother stayed there all the while,
Ministering love with healing hands,
Spinning tales of faraway lands?

What memories will follow them as they go?
All of these, and more, I know.
But most important, can they say,
"She loved God's Word, and taught us to pray"?
—Kathi Macias

# Mothers of the Bible Speak to Mothers of Today

### KATHI MACIAS

NEW HOPE
PUBLISHERS

Birmingham Alabama

New Hope® Publishers
P. O. Box 12065
Birmingham, AL 35202-2065
www.newhopepublishers.com
New Hope Publishers is a division of WMU®

Library of Congress Cataloging-in-Publication Data

Mills-Macias, Kathi, 1948-
  Mothers of the Bible speak to mothers of today / Kathi Macias.
     p. cm.
  ISBN 978-1-59669-215-2 (sc)
  1. Mothers in the Bible. 2. Mothers--Religious life. I. Title.
  BS579.M65M55 2009
  220.9'20852--dc22
                                    2008055233

ISBN-10: 1-59669-215-4
ISBN-13: 978-1-59669-215-2

N084138 • 0409 • 4M1

# Dedication

As always, I dedicate this book to my heavenly Father, who so lovingly and mercifully calls me "daughter," and to His Son, who calls me "forgiven."

I also dedicate this book to my life-partner and best friend, Al, whose shoulder is always there for me when I grow weary.

To the memory of my friend and former agent Sherrill Chidiak, who loved and believed in this book from the beginning, but went home to be with Jesus before it became a reality.

Finally, I dedicate this book to my mother and to all mothers everywhere who seek to fulfill that great calling to *"train up a child in the way he should go"* (Proverbs 22:6). May His love and wisdom guide you each step of the way.

# Contents

### Eve: Without a Role Model
With no one to question or consult, Eve experienced most of the concerns the rest of us mothers have—and then some. Take a fresh look at the "mother of all living"; you'll be surprised at the practical help you'll gain to face your fears and deal with the insecurities synonymous with being a mom.

### Sarah: Mother of Nations
Sometimes God doesn't move as quickly as we desire or respond exactly as we would hope. Sometimes we are tempted to step in to "help" God fulfill His promises (and a mother's desires) for our children. The results: disaster and negative long-term consequences.

### Rebekah: Playing Favorites
It is tough to resist the temptation to cover—or even lie for—a child in order to obtain special treatment or to override negative consequences in that child's life, even when we trust God to work in that child according to His purposes. In this mother's family life, manipulating, maneuvering, deceit, and trickery led to family breakup. God has a better plan for us.

### Rachel and Leah: Competing Through Their Children
We mothers face the temptation of living our lives vicariously through our children, pushing them to excel—and enjoying the bragging rights. We can create or escalate sibling rivalry, as well as foster the idea in our children that they must win—at any cost. Yet, in spite of our failures, all mothers can experience hope, forgiveness, and healing.

### Jochebed: The Greatest Sacrifice
As mothers, we know that the words *mother* and *self-sacrifice* can often be used interchangeably. Our great sacrifice may at times be the most loving and unselfish act a mother can choose for her child, for myriad reasons with far-reaching effects. We see this in the case of Moses's mother.

### Hannah: Woman of Prayer, Gratitude, and Integrity
How many times have we uttered a desperate prayer or proclaimed a selfless oath in the hope of obtaining a particular outcome for our children? When that prayer is answered, it is important to honor our word and our vows regarding our children, even if it involves laying aside our personal dreams and desires.

### Rizpah: Grief-Stricken yet Faithful
Can there be anything more painful to a parent than the death of a child? In addition to the agony, losing a child to death seems to be out of the natural order. Yet, from the beginning, mothers have endured this tragedy, which can result in additional problems: divorce, financial difficulties, and even a loss of faith in God. Yet God sees and cares.

### Bathsheba: Redemption and Restoration
We love our children and are dedicated to their nurture, but do we ever find ourselves haunted by our past as well as feelings of unworthiness? In Bathsheba's life, we see God's amazing faithfulness to forgive and to restore. He does so even when our loss and pain are due to our own mistakes and sins.

### The Widow of Zarephath: Generous to the End

Ever struggle to make ends meet? "Rob Peter to pay Paul"? The widow of Zarephath reminds us that God faithfully provides for our and our children's needs, even in the direst of circumstances, and even beyond our greatest expectations.

### Elizabeth: A Willing Sacrifice

For a mom, life doesn't get much tougher than it was for Elizabeth! We have dreams for our children, but God's plans for them may be different and may even lead them into a more difficult life than we would want. God gives us the strength to make such a great sacrifice.

### The Canaanite Woman: Persevering in Prayer

Every mother who has sought God on behalf of her child, only to despair of God's ever answering, can relate to this determined Canaanite mother. She recognized the Jewish prophet, whom some hailed as the promised Messiah, as a miracle worker, and threw aside conventional restraints of a segregated society. Jesus rewarded her tenacity!

### Salome: Catching the Eternal Vision

We seek God for our children's temporal needs, but do we see their lives from God's point of view? Salome, mother of two of Jesus's disciples, James's and John's, wanted special positions for them. If our hearts' desire is to lead our children to the foot of the Cross—and join them there—we can find great encouragement and direction in her story.

### Eunice and Lois: Passing the Torch
What believing mother hasn't looked at her children and longed to see her own faith burning in their hearts? This chapter's testimony speaks to this, and also to mothers caring for both parents and children, as well as to the issue of a believing mother married to an unbelieving father, yet still managing to raise her children in the fear and admonition of the Lord!

### The Proverbs 31 Woman: A Woman for All Seasons
We mothers often feel we must be all and do all and never get tired. A study of the Proverbs 31 woman, who seems to have mastered such a feat, suggests instead that we may need to approach our lives in seasons. As a result, we may find our husbands and children rising up and calling us blessed!

### Mary: In a Class by Herself
As Mary "pondered in her heart" what God spoke to her regarding her beloved Jesus, we mothers are called to do the same. As Mary allowed Jesus to grow within her, and go into the world, we must allow God's Spirit to bear life in and through us as well. God often calls us as mothers to lay aside our dreams and desires in order to nurture lives that can go forth with that message of forgiveness to a lost and dying world.

*"Mothers reflect God's loving presence on earth."*
**—William R. Webb, educator, US Senator**

"Motherhood—it startles the senses.
It shakes the inner core. It makes the weak strong.
It reaches into the heart and pulls out thorns of
bitterness, fear, and selfishness. It creates wonder
where there is no imagination and softness where
only harshness existed. . . .
It brings floods of tears, mountains of sadness,
valleys of anger, and canyons of frustration.
It brings ridiculous joy; downpours of happiness.
It is the most delightful, painful, and most
life-changing experience."

—Dr. Gail Hayes, author

# Introduction

## TO MOTHERS AND MOTHERS-TO-BE

The Bible relays to us the lives of a multitude of amazing people—among them women who grappled with the issues of motherhood. Many of these individuals would have considered themselves failures as mothers, even as we sometimes do today. Yet God included their varied stories in the Scriptures for several reasons, one of which I'm sure is to help us today to navigate our lives and stand with sure footing as we lead children, grandchildren—even others' children in our communities of caring—down right paths.

If you are or hope to be a mom, no matter how busy you may be, you will want to set aside a few minutes a day to find out what more God wants you to know about motherhood. It is, after all, an honorable position, one designed and appointed to us by our own heavenly Parent. True, the responsibilities of wearing the title of Mom are great, no matter our age—but the rewards are even greater!

I would like to tell you that I decided to write this book to help women deal with some major motherhood issues because I did such a great job of it myself. I'd *like* to tell you that—but I can't, because sometimes I didn't. Instead, I decided it would be a much better idea to write about those "mom issues" by allowing the mothers of the Bible to speak to us, using their life experiences to set the scene and paint the picture.

Included in the picture, you will also find here:

- Thought-provoking quotes about motherhood from a wide spectrum of contemporary and historical individuals, sprinkled throughout the book—some famous, some not
- Key Bible passages for reading about each biblical woman
- Space for you to record your reflections about how you can respond and apply their life lessons, and
- Prayers

Please join me in exploring the lives of these mothers of the Bible, will you? Then listen to what they have to say as you consider your own thoughts on motherhood. I promise, you'll be glad you did—and so will your children, grandchildren, and the other children whose lives you touch now and in the future.

*"There is a woman at the beginning of all great things."*

—Alphonse de Lamartin, French poet, writer, and statesman

# CHAPTER I

# Eve: Without a Role Model

*Then the L*ORD *God made a woman from the rib he had taken out of the man.*
—Genesis 2:22

SUGGESTED SCRIPTURE READINGS:
Genesis 2:18, 21–23; 3:6–7, 11–13, 16; 4:1–5, 8–12, 16, 25

I can think of no more awesome experience than the birth of my first child. At the naive age of 18, this was the most joyous—as well as the most terrifying—occurrence that had ever happened to me. It was as if I were experiencing love for the very first time as I gazed at that precious little life God had entrusted to me. And I thought, *What in the world do I do now? How do I care for him? How do*

*I make sure I'm doing everything right? What if—God forbid—I do something wrong?* Now, two more sons, several grandchildren, and nearly four decades later, I smile at this memory, knowing babies aren't quite as fragile as I'd once imagined. Yet I can't help but wonder how much more challenging and overwhelming motherhood must have been for Eve, who was not only the first woman but also the first mother. What can women today learn about mothering from studying the life of this exiled Garden dweller, who had no role model to imitate, no how-to-be-a-good-mom books to read? Quite a bit, I believe. Let's take a look.

❖ ❖ ❖

Eve, whose name means "life giver," was the only woman ever to become a mother without first having had a mother of her own. In fact, she had no sisters, aunts, grandmothers, or girlfriends to turn to for advice. In short, she had no role models and no one with whom to compare notes.

*She had no sisters, aunts, grandmothers, or girlfriends to turn to for advice.*

She did have Adam, of course, whom, like her, God had made in His image. She had the greatest assortment of pets anyone could ever imagine! And, of course, she had her relationship with God. Yet, as we know from the creation account in Genesis, all of Eve's relationships changed because of sin.

How alone she must have felt once those relationships were no longer perfect. And how frightened and overwhelmed she must have been when her two oldest sons, Cain and Abel, were born, thrusting her into an entirely new realm of responsibility. I am quite sure that more than once throughout the ensuing years, Eve heard God's words echoing in her mind: *"I will greatly increase your pains in childbearing; with pain you will give birth to children"* (Genesis 3:16).

By the time Eve's children were grown and she had experienced the horror of her oldest son murdering his younger brother, she must have realized that the truth of God's words—tying together pain and motherhood—didn't stop at childbirth. This truth remains for mothers today, as we will see as we look at Eve's life before the Fall, immediately afterward, and years later when her children were grown.

## BEFORE THE FALL

The Book of Genesis is a book about beginnings. In fact, the Hebrew word for Genesis, *Bereshit* actually means "in the beginning." The first chapter is about the beginning of creation; the second chapter goes on to tell about the beginning of humankind; the third chapter gives a vivid account of the beginning of sin; and the fourth chapter depicts the tragic and inevitable result of sin's introduction into the human race: the beginning of human conflict.

It all started out so beautifully. When God used Moses to write the creation account in Genesis, He made this clear: *"God created man in his own image, in the image of God he created him; male and female he created **them**"* (Genesis 1:27; emphasis added). The Hebrew root word *tselem*, translated here as *image*, gives the impression that humankind is the only part of God's creation cast in His image.

How perfect Adam and Eve must have been, not only mentally, emotionally, and spiritually, but physically as well. God described the two humans made in His image as *"very good."* God previously had pronounced everything He had made before Adam and Eve as *"good,"* but He reserved *"very good"* to cap off everything culminating in the beginning of humankind. The only aspect of their being that God pronounced as *"not good"* was for man to be alone (see Genesis 2:18).

They lived in an idyllic situation—perfect weather, gorgeous scenery, harmony with the animals, unbroken relationship and fellowship with God, and the absolutely flawless "marriage-made-in-heaven" relationship between one another. Adam and Eve were the original and perfect example of the one-flesh relationship God intended marriage to be. Genesis 2:22 tells us that God made Eve *"from the rib he had taken out of the man."* God could have created Eve from the earth, as He had done with Adam, but He wanted Adam to understand that Eve, unlike the animals created before her, was of the exact same essence as Adam. Adam must have recognized that fact immediately because, as soon as he saw Eve, he said, *"This is now bone of my bones and flesh of my flesh; she shall be called 'woman,' for she was taken out of man"* (Genesis 2:23). Then, following the verse that introduces God's desire for a one-flesh relationship between them, we are told in verse 25, *"The man and his wife were both naked, and they felt no shame."* Not only were Adam and Eve made of the same essence, perfect partners in a perfect relationship, but they were also completely comfortable and unashamed in each other's presence.

They were also comfortable and unashamed in God's presence, for in addition to the perfect one-flesh relationship between Adam and Eve, the two Garden dwellers shared a perfect, ongoing relationship with God. The Creator regularly spent quality time with His creation, as we can easily deduce from Genesis 3:8, immediately following Adam and Eve's fall into sin: *"Then the man and his wife heard the sound of the LORD God as he was walking in the garden in the cool of the day."* Adam and Eve immediately recognized the sound of God's walking in the garden. Why? I would imagine it was because they had heard Him many times before. The three of them—God, Adam, and Eve—had spent time in intimate, direct communion ever since the creation. And, as has always been the case, it was God who came down to commune with them, not the

*Before the Fall, communion between God and those made in His image was as natural as breathing.*

other way around. The Creator always initiates the contact; He is always the One to offer the hand of fellowship first, the One to give of Himself so that a relationship might be restored and maintained between Him and His creation.

Before the Fall, communion between God and those made in His image was as natural as breathing. It was all part of the *"very good"* setting in which Adam and Eve lived. The name *Eden*, by definition, may mean "delight." Adam and Eve had the perfect relationship with each other, with God, and even with the animals. Everything in Eden was "delightful." How was it, then, that these perfect people, introduced into a perfect setting by a perfect God, would soon find themselves hiding from God and even cast out of the Garden?

## IMMEDIATELY AFTER THE FALL

I've heard it remarked that God did not make Eve from Adam's head so she could "lord it over him," nor did He make her from Adam's feet so she could serve as his doormat. God made Eve from Adam's rib so she might walk at his side, next to his heart, as his helper and partner for life. I like that explanation, and it sounds very much like the relationship Adam and Eve enjoyed before the Fall in Genesis 3. But as soon as the serpent entered the picture, everything changed.

The opening verse of this chapter describes the serpent as *"more crafty than any of the wild animals the LORD God had made."* The dictionary defines *crafty* as "skillful, clever; adept in the use of subtlety and cunning; marked by subtlety and guile." The first words out of the serpent's mouth verify this description perfectly, as he said to Eve, *"Did God really say 'You must not eat from any tree in the garden?'"* (Genesis 3:1).

This very cunning creature approached Eve with a challenge to God's words: "Did God *really* say....?" The first temptation recorded in the Bible is the same temptation that assaults us today—an attack on the veracity of God's Word. This serpent was, indeed, crafty, knowing that if he could get Eve to question God's Word, he would have achieved the first step in leading her into rebellion against her Creator.

Now in all fairness to Eve, she immediately caught the serpent's misquoting of God's Word regarding not eating from any tree in the garden. Here is how she responded: *"We may eat fruit from the trees in the garden, but God did say 'You must not eat fruit from the tree that is in the middle of the garden, **and you must not touch it,** or you will die'"* (Genesis 3:2–3; emphasis added). When God gave the command regarding this particular tree, He was speaking directly to Adam, not to Eve, as He had not yet created her. In looking back at the previous chapter, the words God actually spoke to Adam were, *"You are free to eat from any tree in the garden; but you must not eat from the tree of the knowledge of good and evil, for when you eat of it you will surely die"* (Genesis 2:16–17). Did you notice that God didn't say anything about not touching the tree? He merely forbade Adam from eating its fruit, but Eve expanded on God's warning when she spoke to the serpent, saying that they were not even to touch the tree. Whether she did this on her own or whether Adam had added these words when he relayed to Eve God's command regarding the tree, we don't know. Whatever the reason, the serpent ignored the command and instead attacked God's words of consequence.

*"'You will not surely die,' the serpent said to the woman 'For God knows that when you eat of it your eyes will be opened, and you will be like God, knowing good and evil'"* (Genesis 3:4–5). Now the serpent was attacking God on two counts. He was planting seeds of doubt in Eve's mind regarding *the truth of God's Word* and also *the integrity of His character*. The serpent implied that God had not only lied to them, but also that He was trying to hold them back from experiencing something wonderful. Eve's mistake, of course, was listening to these false accusations and then considering them in her mind.

*Satan's methods have changed little since the serpent first confronted Eve.*

Satan, represented by this crafty Garden serpent, continues the same assault today: planting seeds of doubt regarding God's Word and His character in the minds of anyone who will listen. And when that "anyone" is a mother, the consequences are bound to affect her children. Think about it. What are the two fronts on which faith in the one true God, as reflected in the life of a committed Christian, are fought today? The same as in the Garden: God's Word and His character. You may have heard some of the following comments about God's Word and His character; you may even have said them yourself.

- "How can you believe in some ancient book that was written by different authors over a period of hundreds or thousands of years?" (Questioning God's Word)
- "The Bible may contain some great truths and moral guidelines, but you certainly can't take it literally." (Questioning God's Word)
- "How could a loving God allow such awful things to happen in the world?" (Questioning God's character)
- "The Bible is simply a big list of do's and don'ts that God gave us so we wouldn't have any fun or be happy." (Questioning God's character.)

Do you see how Satan's methods have changed little since the serpent first confronted Eve with the temptation to go her own way instead of God's? Yet, because Eve listened, considered, and ultimately gave in to that temptation, everything that had been so perfect and good and delightful in their Garden-of-Eden existence was changed in an instant.

Interestingly enough, however, the Scriptures don't attribute that first sin to Eve, but rather to Adam. *"Sin entered the world through one man* [Adam].... *For just as through the disobedience of the one man* [Adam] *the many were made sinners, so also through the obedience of the one man* [Jesus] *the many will be made righteous"* (Romans 5:12, 19). Why is Adam singled out as having brought sin into the world, rather than Eve? When we look back at Genesis 2 for a moment, right before God gave Adam the warning about not eating from the tree of the knowledge of good and evil, we see that verse 15 says, *"The LORD God took the man and put him in the Garden of Eden to work it and take care of it."* Contrary to what some people suggest, work was not part of the curse that came on mankind after the fall. God gave Adam a job *before* Eve was created; before the encounter between the serpent and the first woman, Adam's assignment from God was to take care of the Garden. He had responsibility for what went on there.

And then came Eve. On her arrival, Adam's responsibilities increased. That doesn't mean that Eve wasn't responsible for her actions, but it may mean that Adam should have been overseeing what took place between Eve and the serpent. He should have stepped in the minute the serpent challenged God's Word and His character, and set that slimy snake straight. Yet he didn't, even though he was right there when it all happened. When Eve yielded to the serpent's temptation to disobey God and eat from the forbidden tree, she also gave some of the fruit *"to her husband, who was with her, and he ate it"* (Genesis 3:6).

Tragic. The very man God had so lovingly created and placed in charge of the Garden now willingly and knowingly chose with Eve to disobey God and subjugate himself—and all his descendents—to the serpent, the devil, the one who had deceived Eve and now led both of them into rebellion against their Creator. And that's the key: Eve was deceived, while Adam knew more clearly what he was doing, and so *he* is named in Scripture as the one who brought sin into the world.

The Apostle Paul, in writing to the church at Corinth, warned about the universality of Eve's deception when he said, *"But I am afraid that **just as Eve was deceived by the serpent's cunning,** your minds may somehow be led astray from your sincere and pure devotion to Christ"* (2 Corinthians 11:3; emphasis added). Throughout history, the deceiver continues to tempt and draw people into rebellion against their Creator by challenging the truth of God's Word and the goodness of His character. Eve was the first to be deceived, but she certainly wasn't the last.

## THROUGH THE EYES OF SIN

Can you imagine how Eve must have felt when the consequences of her disobedience began to surface? The first realization of the enormity of their sin came immediately after they yielded to temptation and ate the fruit. Genesis 3:7 declares, *"Then the eyes of both of them were opened, and they realized they were naked."* Before they sinned they were naked; they simply didn't realize it because God had pronounced everything about them, including their nakedness, as *"very good."* Now, suddenly, they were seeing things they hadn't seen before. Whereas, before their sin, they saw themselves and their surroundings only as God saw them—as He had created them, pure and sinless—they now saw through the eyes of sin. Instantly they were ashamed and began looking for a way to cover themselves: *"They sewed fig leaves together and made coverings for themselves"* (Genesis 3:7).

This was the first attempt at man-made religion—human beings attempting to cover their sins through their own efforts. And yet we know it didn't work (and still doesn't), for the very next time God came to the Garden to walk with them as He had done in the past, Adam told God, *"I heard you in the garden, and I was afraid because I was naked; so I hid"* (Genesis 3:10). If their attempt at self-covering had been enough, they would not have been afraid of God and would not have hidden themselves from Him.

Can you imagine a sadder scene? These two previously perfect human beings—in perfect relationship with God and with each other, living in perfect surroundings—were now hiding in shame and fear from their Creator. Intimate relationship with God had been broken and their relationship with each other damaged, as we see when God asked Adam if he had eaten from the forbidden tree. Did Adam, who had willingly and knowingly disobeyed God, admit his wrong and ask for God's forgiveness for himself and his wife, whose disobedience was due to her own deception and Adam's failure to intervene? No, he didn't. Instead he shifted the blame, first to Eve, and then to God!

*Adam blamed not only Eve for his sin, but God as well!*

*"The woman you put here with me—she gave me some fruit from the tree, and I ate it"* (Genesis 3:12). *"The woman you put here with me...."* In effect, Adam was saying, "It was her fault, God—Eve's. You know, that woman *You* put here with me." Translation: "It's not my fault. If You hadn't put Eve here, I never would have sinned." Adam blamed not only Eve for his sin, but God as well! At least Eve was honest enough when she was confronted to admit to God, *"The serpent deceived me, and I ate"* (Genesis 3:13).

Try to picture for a moment what Eve must have been experiencing at that instant. First, her once-perfect relationship with God had been broken, and now her beloved husband had turned on her in an attempt to save himself. Could their love survive such an onslaught? Could she ever trust or respect him again? Standing there in her shame and heartache and hand-sewn fig-leaf covering, she could have felt more helpless and hopeless than any other human being down through the ages.

But then, after pronouncing His curse against these two mutineers, God graciously and mercifully disproved everything the serpent had said about Him: He showed His Word to be true and His character perfect. In His infinite love and mercy, God instituted the first blood-sacrifice and clothed Adam and Eve in animal skins. Though He would banish them from the Garden of Eden because of their sin, He had also exhibited to them that He would one day provide a Redeemer, a Savior to open the door for the human race to be restored to the once-perfect relationship with God that had now been lost in the Garden rebellion.

Amazingly, it is at this point that Adam named his wife Eve, *"because she would become the mother of all the living"* (Genesis 3:20). In the midst of the most far-reaching tragedy of all time, Adam found a reason to be optimistic about the future. That optimism was born not only out of his belief that God would one day redeem mankind, but also out of the thought that Eve would soon become a mother—possibly even of the Redeemer Himself.

And so, in Genesis 4, we see Adam's hope realized as he *"lay with his wife Eve, and she became pregnant and gave birth to Cain. She said 'With the help of the LORD I have brought forth a man.' Later she gave birth to his brother Abel"* (Genesis 4:1–2). Living now outside the Garden and apart from daily communion with God, Eve fulfilled the name Adam had given her and became a life-giver. Yet even in her now-fallen state, banished from Eden and dealing for the first time with the effects of sin, Eve did not forget God. She acknowledged that it was only with the help of the "LORD" that she had been able to bring forth new life. So it is with all of us who are privileged to be called mothers, whether through conception and birth, adoption, foster care, or otherwise.

Now that my sons are all grown and married with families of their own, I can look back on their growing-up years and remember some definitely tough times mixed in with the good. However, I have to admit that I can't even begin to imagine the type of heartache Eve must have endured when her firstborn murdered his younger brother. Losing a child under any circumstance is devastating, but to lose a child at the murderous hand of his or her sibling is nearly incomprehensible to me.

Yet that is what happened. The Genesis account doesn't give us any information on Cain and Abel's childhood. The story simply jumps from their birth straight to their adulthood when Cain worked as a farmer and Abel as a shepherd. We then see in Genesis 4:3 that *"in the course of time"* Cain and Abel each brought an offering to the Lord. Before we examine their specific offerings, we need to ask ourselves *why* they brought offerings to God. The most logical assumption at that point is that Adam and Eve had instructed them to do so.

> *Sibling rivalry is as old as Cain and Abel, and it is a common theme that runs through the Bible.*

Though we have no specific recorded dialogue between Adam and Eve and their offspring, Cain and Abel's actions of bringing offerings to God point to the fact that their parents did their best to raise them to honor and respect their Creator.

We can also assume that, as most parents, Adam and Eve told stories to their sons about how life had been before their births, before the Fall, when they had experienced that perfect, idyllic life in Eden until the serpent led *them* into rebellion and disobedience against God. In the telling of those stories, the boys no doubt heard that God Himself had instituted the first blood sacrifice, establishing the precedent for acceptable offerings. That's where Cain got into trouble.

Hebrews 9:22 tells us: *"Without the shedding of blood there is no forgiveness."* Cain must have known this. His parents had instructed both him and Abel in what constituted an acceptable offering to God. They had told their sons how, after they had sinned, they had tried to cover themselves with fig leaves, but God had rejected their feeble attempt and taken care of the situation Himself by slaughtering an animal and covering them with its skin. There was no reason for Cain to believe that his own attempt at man-made religion would be any more acceptable to God than had his parents' botched episode with the fig leaves. But he did it anyway, and the consequences were nearly as horrific as his parents' banishment from the Garden.

Sibling rivalry *is* as old as Cain and Abel, and it is a common theme that runs through the Bible. Any of us who have more than one child—or grew up with brothers and sisters of our own—have seen the effects of sibling rivalry firsthand. The case with Cain and Abel, however, must have been extreme for Cain's jealousy and resentment of Abel to escalate to the point of such violence. When God voiced His approval of Abel's blood sacrifice from the flocks and rejected Cain's bloodless offering from the fields, the disobedient and rebellious young man went right over the edge, even though he knew beforehand that God would not accept an offering that required no bloodshed.

Was he testing God, hoping to change the Creator's mind? Did Cain reason that his offering was as acceptable as Abel's because both came from the fruit of their labors? The Scriptures don't answer those questions directly, and yet there is an implied *yes* in Cain's behavior, particularly when God confronted him on his presumptuous offering.

*"Why are you angry?"* God asked him. *"If you do what is right, will you not be accepted?"* (Genesis 4:6–7). Through God's questions to Cain we can conclude that the young man knew what was right, and yet had chosen to do otherwise. Yet, instead of repenting and asking God's forgiveness, Cain invited his brother out into the field. *"And while they were in the field, Cain attacked his brother Abel and killed him"* (Genesis 4:8).

Cold, premeditated murder, born out of hot, jealous hatred—and still Cain refused to repent. When God asked him where Abel was, Cain replied, *"I don't know. Am I my brother's keeper?"* (Genesis 4:9).

Thus Cain was cursed, banished from the Lord's presence and from the home where he had grown up. In one day's time, Adam and Eve lost both their children. It is hard to imagine

*God was the perfect role model to her, as He is to all parents who feel inadequate for the task set before them.*

how they could go on after experiencing such heartache, and yet we know they did. Genesis 4:25 tells us that Eve again became pregnant and gave birth to another son, whom she named Seth, and she said, *"God has granted me another child in place of Abel, since Cain killed him."* The amazing thing about this part of the story is that it was through Seth's bloodline that God's Redeemer—Jesus, the promised Messiah—was born. Even after suffering incredible loss, Eve became the "mother of all living," even as Adam had prophesied when he named her, before they were driven out of the Garden of Eden.

Though Eve had no human role model to help her in her trials, God was the perfect role model to her, as He is to all parents who feel inadequate for the task set before them. It was God who came down to Adam and Eve to commune with them in the Garden. It was God who shed blood to provide a temporary covering for their sin. And it was God who helped them bring forth sons and daughters to populate the earth and eventually to produce a Redeemer.

*"Motherhood is the greatest privilege of life."*
—**May Coker, author**

## SOMETHING TO THINK ABOUT/
## ENTER IN YOUR JOURNAL:

1. It has been said that deciding to have a child is like deciding to let your heart walk around outside your body for the rest of your life. How does that saying apply to Eve's life, and maybe even to yours?

2. How does this story of the first dysfunctional family affect your understanding of Proverbs 22:6: *"Train a child in the way he should go, and when he is old he will not turn from it"?*

3. How does knowing that God was Eve's perfect parental role model help you face your challenges of motherhood?

*"We can't order our children 'rare' or 'well-done.' We take them as God gives them to us."*
**—Elaine Miller, author**

# A MOTHER'S PRAYER

*Thank You, Lord, that You are my Father. Thank You that You love me and want what's best for me and for my children. Help me, Lord, to keep my eyes and heart focused on You, trusting You to make me the mother You want me to be. In Jesus's name. Amen.*

**"A partnership with God is motherhood."**
**—Author unknown**

*"Happiness is something that happens to you, but contentment in mothering is something you choose."*

—Kathy Collard Miller, author

# CHAPTER 2

# Sarah: Mother of Nations

*Now Sarai, Abram's wife, had borne him no children. And she had an Egyptian maidservant whose name was Hagar.... And the LORD visited Sarah as He had said, and the LORD did for Sarah as He had spoken.*
—Genesis 16:1; 21:1

SUGGESTED SCRIPTURE READINGS:
Genesis 11:29–31; 12:5, 11–20; 16:1–8; 17:15–21; 18:6–15; 20:2, 14–18; 21:1–12; 23:1–2, 19; 24:36, 67; 25:10–12; 49:31; Isaiah 51:2; Romans 4:19; 9:9; Hebrews 11:11; 1 Peter 3:6

The Scriptures tell us that Sarah was a beautiful woman, as well as a woman who had received a powerful promise from God. But it seems Sarah was also impatient. She tired of waiting for God to fulfill

His promise and decided to "help Him out." The results were disastrous, and the fallout continued through the centuries.

And yet, can't most of us relate to Sarah and her impatience? I know I can, especially when I think about how long she waited. How many times I have become weary with waiting on God to fulfill His Word, and instead have jumped in and tried to fix and manipulate things on my own! How did it turn out? If you're anything like me—or Sarah—you already know the answer. Then again, maybe Sarah wasn't quite as hasty as she might first appear.

❖ ❖ ❖

When we first meet Sarah, approximately 2,000 years before the birth of Christ, she is called *Sarai*, and she lives with her husband, Abram, in a city called Ur in what is now southern Iraq. Though Ur's glory days were fading, it was still the site of a flourishing and prosperous society, and the couple enjoyed the fruits of a privileged life, as well as a love-filled and committed marriage—and yet they were childless.

This was no small thing in those days and in that society, and Sarai knew it. Though her name evidently contained the meaning of "princess," she must have wondered why the Prince whose name she bore didn't remove her curse and bless her with children.

It is around this very dilemma that Sarai and Abram's life revolved, and it didn't become any easier when God told them to leave behind everything they knew and go to an unknown land that He would show them and where He would bless them. With a command to leave and a promise of blessing as their marching orders, Sarai and Abram ventured forth into an adventure far beyond anything they could begin to imagine.

## THE CALL, THE PROMISE…AND THE JOURNEY

Sarai was more than an obedient wife; she was also a trusting one. She obviously trusted her husband, but she must also have trusted the invisible God he worshipped. It cannot have been an easy adjustment to have Abram come to her and tell her that God had spoken to him and said:

> *"Get out of your country, from your family and from your father's house, to a land that I will show you. I will make you a great nation; I will bless you and make your name great; and you shall be a blessing. I will bless those who bless you, and I will curse him who curses you; and in you all the families of the earth shall be blessed."*
> —Genesis 12:1–3

For one thing, God wasn't in the habit of speaking to people in Ur—at least, not as far as Sarai knew—and for another thing, obeying this "message" from Abram's unseen God would necessitate a complete uprooting of their entire life. True, it was quite a lofty promise that God had tossed into the mix, but leave behind country, family, friends...everything comfortable and familiar? That was asking a lot.

But Sarai was not only obedient and trusting, she was also very much Abram's partner. She and Abram might have been married for at least four decades at this point, and their separate lives had long since become one. When the call from God invaded their lives, Sarai was still a stunningly beautiful woman, though she was already in her sixties and no doubt more than slightly set in her ways. She was particularly accustomed to a relatively luxurious life, so packing up and leaving her comfortable home to follow her husband through the desert to some unknown destination must have greatly challenged her love and faith.

*She was already in her sixties and no doubt more than slightly set in her ways.*

Yet she went. Loyal to her husband and trusting that what Abram claimed to have heard from God would truly come to pass, she pulled up stakes, kissed her loved ones goodbye, and set her heart to follow after an invisible God and her husband's belief in His call...and His promise.

The journey took longer and entailed more adventures than Sarai could possibly have anticipated, even in her wildest dreams. "Are we there yet?" must have been the question of the day—every day—and not just for Sarai but also for all who traveled with them. For though God instructed Abram to leave his father's family and his house, Abram's nephew Lot, as well as *"all their possessions that they had gathered and the people whom they had acquired"* went with them.

It must have been quite a caravan that headed out from the heart of this ancient city, as Abram was considered a wealthy man with many possessions and servants. I imagine there was more than a bit of fanfare as they departed—not to mention a lot of tears, as they said goodbye to friends and loved ones, unsure if they would ever see them again.

Yet in obedience they left, traveling north along an ancient trade route that followed the Euphrates River. After a stop in Haran, they turned south and moved on to Canaan. The vast majority of the remainder of their lives was spent wandering in that sparsely populated area.

Much of the land through which Abram and Sarai and their entourage passed was desolate at best, dangerous at worst. Still, they continued on. They hadn't gone far on their journey when Abram stopped and built an altar to the Lord in the valley of Shechem. He later built another altar in Bethel, 12 miles north of Jerusalem, and then another under an oak at Mamre. Though we are not told that Sarai worshipped at these altars with her husband, it is easy to imagine that she did, since Peter, in the New Testament, refers to Sarai (whom the apostle later called Sarah, the name God had given her) as an *"heir"* with Abram (whom Peter called Abraham) to *"the grace of life"* (1 Peter 3:7).

*A lot of manipulation and mayhem entered the picture, causing problems of generational magnitude.*

Through times of prosperity and peace, of adversity and danger, Sarai followed Abram, who followed the call and the promise of

God. They traveled on a lifelong journey together that eventually took them to the fulfillment of God's promise to make Abram and Sarai the father and mother of many nations—but not before a lot of manipulation and mayhem entered the picture, causing problems of generational magnitude.

## THE COMPROMISE

Despite many harrowing incidents along the way, the real problem didn't arise until about ten years after Abram and Sarai arrived in Canaan. How many long hours of caravanning around the wilderness and staring up at the stars at night had Sarai spent; wondering when this God who had called them on their journey would finally come through and fulfill His promise to make Abram "a great nation"? And how could that happen unless she and Abram had a child? And how could they have a child unless God had intervened and miraculously granted them one, since they were both getting far past the normal age of childbearing?

That being said, to Sarai's credit, she *did* wait for a full ten years before finally deciding to take matters into her own hands. After all, maybe they had misunderstood this invisible God. Maybe, rather than waiting for a miraculous conception, they were supposed to take advantage of the custom of the day, which was to provide a sort of surrogate heir when a husband and wife were unable to produce one of their own. In other words, when a wife couldn't perform her to duty to her husband by producing a son, she could provide an heir for him by granting to him one of her own women servants, with whom the husband would then have sexual relations. If those relations resulted in the birth of a child, that child would legally belong to the husband and wife, rather than to the servant who bore the child.

This concession was no small decision for Sarai. Not only was this an admission that all hope of conceiving and bearing her own child was gone, but also it was a willing physical sharing of the man she loved with another woman. Even to fulfill her longing and duty to have a child, she must have wrestled long and hard before making such a heart-wrenching decision.

However, what was the alternative? How many more years should she and Abram wait for something that very obviously—to her—was not going to happen? And with each day they waited, the more impossible the situation appeared. Neither of them was getting any younger, and everyone knew that old women—even one who was still as beautiful as Sarai—could not produce a child.

Thus the Bible tells us, in desperation Sarai looked to her maidservant Hagar, who was an Egyptian, and decided to give her to Abram to conceive and bear the promised heir and thus start the "great nation" promised to them by God. Here is how the Bible tells us that Sarai explained her decision to Abram: *"See now, the Lord has restrained me from bearing children. Please, go in to my maid; perhaps I shall obtain children by her"* (Genesis 16:2).

As a wife, I can only imagine how painful it must have been for Sarai to speak those words to the man she loved. For that reason, even though I realize she should have remained patient and waited on God, my heart goes out to her. And then, when Abram *"heeded the voice of Sarai"* (Genesis 16:2) and took her up on her offer, the poor woman must have been in agony. If she thought she'd had sleepless nights before, lying awake and wondering when God would fulfill His promise to give them a child, how much worse must it have been on the nights when she lay alone in her tent, knowing her husband was sharing a bed with another woman?

Finally, however, the announcement was made: Hagar was pregnant, and Abram would finally have a child. That should have taken the pressure off everyone and produced a lot of joy and excitement in the camp—and maybe it did, at least initially. But then Hagar's attitude changed. Genesis 16:4 tells us that *"when she [Hagar] saw that she had conceived, her mistress [Sarai] became despised in her eyes."*

*Once Hagar realized she had done what her mistress had been unable to do, she began to look upon Sarai with contempt.*

Undoubtedly Hagar had been a dutiful and submissive servant before Sarai gave her to Abram, but once Hagar realized she had done what her mistress had been unable to do—conceive a child by the master—she began to look upon Sarai with contempt. Suddenly Sarai wasn't so sure she had made the right decision after all. *"My wrong be upon you,"* she said to Abram. *"I gave my maid into your embrace; and when she saw that she had conceived, I became despised in her eyes. The LORD judge between you and me"* (Genesis 16:5).

Poor Abram! First his wife tells him to go sleep with Hagar so he can get her pregnant and finally produce the long-awaited son, and now Sarai is mad at him for doing so. But was Abram entirely innocent in this unwise decision to try to short-circuit God's promise? Not really. After all, it was to Abram God made the promise, and the promise included Sarai, not Sarai's maid. Abram could very easily have said no to his wife's suggestion and continued to wait on God . . . but he didn't. Instead, he answered her this way: *"Indeed your maid is in your hand; do to her as you please"* (Genesis 16:6).

Now we've got to be thinking, "Poor Hagar!" She's the one who had no say in this situation, and now she's at the mercy of an angry and jealous wife. Of course, if she hadn't let her pride get in the way and had maintained a humble and submissive attitude toward her mistress, she might not have found herself in such a predicament.

As it was, Sarai *"dealt harshly"* with Hagar, and Hagar *"fled from her presence"* into the wilderness (Genesis 16:6), where she had an unexpected visit from the Angel of the Lord (Genesis 16:7), the very same God who had given the promise to Abram and Sarai to bring from them a "great nation." After a conversation between the Angel of the Lord and Hagar, in which God instructed her to return to Sarai and submit to her, He then gave this young Egyptian maid a great promise of her own:

*"I will multiply your descendants exceedingly, so that they shall not be counted for multitude." And the Angel of the LORD said to her: 'Behold, you are with child, and you shall bear a son. You shall call his name Ishmael, because the LORD has heard your affliction. He shall be a wild man; his hand shall be against every man, and every man's*

*hand against him, and he shall dwell in the presence of all his brethren.'"*
—Genesis 16:10–12

God had promised that this offspring of Abram and Hagar, whom they were to name Ishmael, would also become a great multitude of people, characterized by a certain wildness and a high level of conflict. But their primary feelings of animosity would be directed at the promised one yet to be born to Abram and Sarai.

And so Hagar returned to the camp, and when Abram was 86 years old, Ishmael was born (Genesis 16:16). Though we have no clear record of what took place over the next 13 years, we can only assume from facts that are recorded later that Abram came to love Ishmael very much. We can also assume that Sarai and Hagar established some sort of peace between them because when we fast-forward to the next mention of this intertwined group, Abram is 99 years old, and they are all still living together in the same camp. It is then, more than two decades after God first issued His call and His promise to Abram, when God appeared and spoke to him again. *"I am Almighty God; walk before Me and be blameless,"* God instructed Abram. *"And I will make My covenant between Me and you, and will multiply you exceedingly"* (Genesis 17:1–2).

I'm not surprised that the Bible then tells us that Abram *"fell on his face"* before the Lord (Genesis 17:3). After all, not only was he being visited by God Himself, but Abram knew he hadn't waited for God to fulfill His promise but instead had rushed ahead to try to fulfill it himself. He must have been terrified as he lay there, face in the dirt, waiting to hear what God would say to him next.

*"As for Me, behold, My covenant is with you, and you shall be a father of many nations. No longer shall your name be called Abram, but your name shall be Abraham; for I have made you a father of many nations. I will make you exceedingly fruitful; and I will make nations of you, and kings shall come from you. And I will establish My covenant between Me and you and your descendants after you in their generations, for an everlasting covenant, to be*

*God to you and your descendants after you. Also I give to you and your descendants after you the land in which you are a stranger, all the land of Canaan, as an everlasting possession; and I will be their God.... As for Sarai your wife, you shall not call her name Sarai, but Sarah shall be her name. And I will bless her and also give you a son by her; then I will bless her, and she shall be a mother of nations; kings of peoples shall be from her."*
—Genesis 17:4–8, 15–16

Though God had confirmed His promise, as well as the fact that the promised heir would come through Sarah and not Hagar, Abraham, who loved Ishmael, tried to bargain with God on Ishmael's behalf. God would have none of it. The promise would come through the legitimate son that would be born to Abraham's wife, not his concubine, though God did assure Abraham that He would extend a certain level of blessing to Ishmael and his descendants as well.

> *God did assure Abraham that He would extend a certain level of blessing to Ishmael and his descendants.*

*"But My covenant I will establish with Isaac,"* God told Abraham, even establishing the promised son's name, *"whom Sarah shall bear to you at this set time next year"* (Genesis 17:21).

And so it was established. The promise was still a promise, and it would come to pass in a year—not through the Egyptian maid's son, Ishmael, but through a son named Isaac, who was yet to be conceived by Abraham's legitimate wife, Sarah. God had even established new names for Abram and Sarai. *Abram*, meaning "exalted father," would now be called *Abraham*, meaning "father of many [nations]," and *Sarai*, perhaps meaning "Yahweh is Prince," would now be called *Sarah*, meaning "princess."

God also established the covenant of circumcision with Abraham and his descendants on that day, and Abraham quickly followed through, having all the males of his household, including himself and Ishmael, circumcised as a sign of his covenant with God.

# THE FULFILLMENT

Ah, at last, the promise was about to be fulfilled, and all would be peaceful in the camp—or not. Though Sarah, then 90, and Abraham, 100, rejoiced at the birth of their son, Isaac, not everyone was quite so excited. Abraham undoubtedly continued to love Hagar's child, Ishmael, but the boy was no longer the favorite son or the rightful heir.

Then, when Isaac was three or four, the time when children were traditionally weaned, Abraham threw a great party to celebrate the event. During the celebration, Sarah spotted Ishmael teasing or scoffing at Isaac, and being a typical protective mother, did not like that one bit.

*"Cast out this bondwoman and her son,"* she said to Abraham, *"for the son of this bondwoman shall not be heir with my son, namely with Isaac"* (Genesis 21:10). Sarah wanted to make it perfectly clear that she considered her son the only heir, the only legitimate son, and that Ishmael had no part in the inheritance or promise of God. The Bible says that Sarah's words were *"very displeasing in Abraham's sight because of his son"* (Genesis 21:11).

Again we see that Abraham loved Ishmael and didn't want to disinherit him, even though he knew that Isaac was the rightful heir. Yet God, in His infinite mercy and goodness, spoke again to Abraham and assured him that although Sarah was right and the promise was to be established only through Isaac, God would still bless Ishmael and *"make a nation of the son of the bondwoman, because he is your seed"* (Genesis 21:13). And so, once again acting in obedience to God, Abraham *"rose early in the morning, and took bread and a skin of water; and putting it on her [Hagar's] shoulder, he gave it and the boy to Hagar, and sent her away. Then she departed and wandered in the Wilderness of Beersheba"* (Genesis 21:14).

How this must have grieved Abraham, and how it must have terrified Hagar and Ishmael! Yet the remainder of the chapter shows that God, as always, was faithful to His promise and provided for Hagar and Ishmael.

However, if Abraham thought turning Hagar and Ishmael out of the camp was difficult, the real test was yet to come. In Genesis 22 we see where God speaks to Abraham again, this time commanding him to take his son—*"your only son Isaac, whom you love"* (Genesis 22:2)—and offer him up as a burnt offering to God.

OK, if I'm Sarah, I've got a serious problem at this point. I waited 90 years to have a son, and now God wants my husband to kill him. Over my dead body—or his—but not my son's! No way. That would be taking obedience and submission too far, don't you think?

Which also makes me think that Abraham didn't tell Sarah about God's latest word to him. In fact, Sarah isn't even mentioned in Genesis 22, and I can't help but believe that's exactly the reason.

*His faith [was] in the promise of God that a great nation would come through Isaac; therefore, he had to believe that God had a plan—even though Abraham didn't have a clue what it was.*

Abraham *"rose early in the morning and saddled his donkey, and took two of his young men with him, and Isaac his son; and he split the wood for the burnt offering, and arose and went to the place of which God had told him"* (Genesis 22:3). Perhaps he went early so he wouldn't have to explain to Sarah what he was doing. Abraham knew his wife well; he knew she was faithful and dutiful and obedient. He also knew she had her limits—and this was most likely one of them.

He set out very early to carry out the deed God had commanded him to perform. It is here that we see one of the earliest and clearest portrayals of God offering up His own Son, Jesus, 2,000 years later. As Abraham, with heart so heavy it must have weighed the poor man's feet down like lead, trudged along, Isaac had a question for him: *"Look, the fire and the wood, but where is the lamb for a burnt offering?"* (Genesis 22:7) And then came one of the greatest statements of faith ever made: *"My son, God will provide for Himself the lamb for a burnt offering"* (Genesis 22:8).

Abraham was placing all his faith in the promise of God that a great nation would come through Isaac; therefore, he had to believe that God had a plan—even though Abraham didn't have a clue what it was. Yet even if it meant God would have to raise Isaac from the dead to fulfill His promise, Abraham believed He would do it.

Abraham was poised to plunge the knife into his beloved son's heart when the Angel of the Lord stopped him. *"Do not lay your hand on the lad, or do anything to him; for now I know that you fear God, seeing you have not withheld your son, your only son, from Me"* (Genesis 22:12).

Then Abraham *"lifted his eyes and looked, and there behind him was a ram caught in a thicket by its horns. So Abraham went and took the ram, and offered it up for a burnt offering instead of his son"* (Genesis 22:13). God truly had *"provide[d] for Himself the lamb for a burnt offering,"* as Abraham had told Isaac that He would do. And so Abraham *"called the name of the place, The-Lord-Will-Provide; as it is said to this day, 'In the Mount of the Lord it shall be provided'"* (Genesis 22:14).

When God spoke again, it was to bless Abraham and all those who would be descended from him:

> *"By Myself I have sworn," says the Lord, "because you have done this thing, and have not withheld your son, your only son—blessing I will bless you, and multiplying I will multiply your descendants as the stars of the heaven and as the sand which is on the seashore; and your descendants shall possess the gate of their enemies. In your seed all the nations of the earth shall be blessed, because you have obeyed My voice."*
> —Genesis 22:16–18

So the promise has continued through the centuries, as has the enmity between the descendants of Ishmael and Isaac.

As for Sarah, she lived to the ripe old age of 127, after which Abraham buried her and mourned over her for many days. It was obvious this couple shared a great love for one another, and Isaac was the product of that love and God's promise. Dear Sarah, though 90 years old when her only child was born, had the joy and privilege of watching him grow to adulthood, though she no doubt lived with regret over not having waited on God to fulfill His promise instead of giving her Egyptian maidservant to her husband and having to deal with the aftermath of that relationship and its consequences.

Sarah also has the honor of being listed in the "hall of faith" chapter of Hebrews, where it is said of her:

> *By faith Sarah herself also received strength to conceive seed, and she bore a child when she was past the age, because she judged Him faithful who had promised. Therefore from one man, and him as good as dead, were born as many as the stars of the sky in multitude—innumerable as the sand which is by the seashore."*
> —Hebrews 11:11–12

Though Sarah and Abraham grew impatient and faltered in their faith, as many of us do, they returned to walk in the promises of God, and as a result became known as the father and mother of many nations, including and especially God's chosen people, Israel.

> *"Motherhood is a major faith-walk.*
> *My kids would never have survived without*
> *that hot line to heaven for guidance!"*
> —**Annetta Dillinger, author, speaker**

## SOMETHING TO THINK ABOUT/
## ENTER IN YOUR JOURNAL:

1. In reading about Sarah's life before she and Abraham left Ur, as well as the many years they wandered in the wilderness while she awaited the fulfillment of God's promise to give them a son, how might your feelings have changed toward her and the decision she made regarding Hagar?

2. What situations in your own life mirror Sarah's "Hagar decision" to abandon God's best and settle for something less?

3. In thinking about the generational repercussions of Sarah's decision, what can you do in your own life to help ensure that your own descendants will walk in blessing, rather than in turmoil and enmity?

*"No man is poor who has a godly mother."*
—**Abraham Lincoln, US President**

## A MOTHER'S PRAYER:

*Father, give us hearts that are willing to seek You, to wait on You, and to continue to walk in the truth and promises You have given us. In Jesus's name. Amen.*

**"He who takes a child by the hand takes a mother by the heart."**
**—Proverb**

*"God makes it hard to be a mother."*

—Lynda Allison Doty, author

# CHAPTER 3

# Rebekah: Playing Favorites

*Before he [Abraham's servant, Eliezer] had finished praying, Rebekah came out with her jar on her shoulder.... The girl was very beautiful, a virgin.*
—Genesis 24:15, 16

SUGGESTED SCRIPTURE READINGS:
Genesis 23:17–20; 24:1–4, 58, 66–67; 25:20–28; 27:6–12; 28:5

As a mother, have you ever been tempted to cover or even lie for your child in order to obtain special treatment or to override negative consequences in that child's life, rather than trusting the Lord to work according to His purposes? Have you ever been involved in a family situation where there were "favorites" among siblings? Though this chapter depicts Rebekah as a loving wife and mother of twin boys, she ends up favoring the younger son, while her husband favors the elder. This results in a lot of manipulating and maneuvering, as well as downright deceit and trickery, which literally leads to the physical breakup of the family. It is a tragic story, with much to speak to us in similar situations today.

❖ ❖ ❖

Rebekah is first introduced to us, literally, on "the wings of a prayer." As Abraham's servant Eliezer later told Rebekah's brother Laban, *"Before I finished praying in my heart, Rebekah came out"* (Genesis 24:45). In a setting of romance and purity, bathed in prayer, this beautiful virgin girl, fulfilling the mundane task of drawing water for herself and her family, appears and steps into her God-ordained destiny, agreeing to marry Abraham's son Isaac eventually becoming one of the great matriarchs of the Bible. It is an idyllic, scriptural way for a marriage to begin, but—as many of us can attest—our lives and relationships haven't always begun with or followed such a perfect pattern.

Now before you think Rebekah's life can't possibly have any relevance for your own, consider the fact that this young woman experienced many trials and heartaches in the fulfillment of her life's calling as wife and mother. Let's take a look at Rebekah—where she came from, how she ended up where she did, and the price she paid for some of the decisions she made in her life.

## THE PAST

Keeping in mind that Abraham, Isaac, and Jacob are considered the three patriarchs of the Jewish people, we see here in Genesis 23 the first recorded Jewish burial, as Abraham purchases the land in which to bury his beloved wife, Sarah. Then, in the very next chapter, we have the first recorded Jewish wedding, in that a matchmaker was involved in bringing together the bride and groom. The use of a matchmaker to arrange marriages is a practice that was followed by Jewish people for many generations, primarily as a means of establishing a suitable union based on mutual understanding and interests, and also to prevent intermarriage with non-Jews, a practice forbidden throughout the Old Testament.

So why did Abraham ask his servant to go back to his native country and find a wife for Isaac among his own relatives? Why was he so adamant about his son's not marrying one of the Canaanite women among whom he now lived? After all, God had called Abraham to leave his homeland and his relatives behind in order to fulfill God's purposes for him. Abraham had obeyed, and he now lived in a pagan society. And yet, was his own family any different?

Not really. Abraham's relatives were also pagans, in that they did not worship the true God (see Joshua 24:2). Yet history tells us that the moral degradation of the Canaanite society far exceeded anything practiced or tolerated in the land of Abraham's origin. In addition, a girl from a distant land was less likely to fall into the exceedingly sinful lifestyle of the Canaanites, and more likely to adopt and follow Isaac's religious beliefs, joining with him to shine as lights in the darkness, even as God had called them to do.

*Rebekah is introduced as a beautiful young virgin...she was not yet a worshipper of the true God.*

Implied in Abraham's choice, of course, was that by choosing a wife for Isaac from the less morally corrupt society of his youth, his grandchildren would have a much better chance of growing up to fear and worship the true God. In other words, since there were no other true believers from which to choose a wife for his son, Abraham resorted to trying to find the most moral wife possible. For that, he sent his servant back to the home and people of his childhood.

We see that, although Rebekah is introduced to us as a beautiful young virgin, appearing on the scene as an answer to prayer, she was not yet a worshipper of the true God. Yet Abraham sent his representative to choose her as Isaac's wife.

There is something very meaningful and sacred for all of us in this method of choosing a bride. When God calls, or "chooses" us,

He sends His Holy Spirit to woo us, to set up the joining together of our lives to that of His Son, Jesus. Before that happens, we are, for the most part, living as pagans in a pagan society, not worshipping the true God. Some of us weren't even close to being beautiful, chaste virgins in the natural *or* moral sense when we became betrothed, or engaged, to God. Yet He chose us anyway, knowing that His beauty and His purity would cover us and, eventually, change us into what He had purposed for us—to be joined together with Him in order to shine as lights in the darkness.

> *The most important thing to remember about the past is not that it was good or evil, but that it is past.*

However, before Rebekah could join with Isaac in marriage and fulfill her destiny, she had to agree to become his wife, as expressed in Genesis 24:58. The matchmaker had come to ask her to return with him to marry his master's son, though Rebekah had the option of refusing to leave her family and homeland. In much the same way, when the Holy Spirit comes to woo us, to call us to join ourselves to Jesus in an eternal love relationship, we must say yes to His proposal before we are joined together with Him forever, ready to move into all that He has purposed for us. If you have never said yes to Jesus, will you pray this prayer right now? The Matchmaker is waiting for your answer.

> *Dear Lord, I thank You for the great love that sent Your Son to die in my place, and now has sent Your Spirit to call me to Yourself. I accept Your invitation, Lord. I want to belong to You forever. I am placing my faith in Christ for eternal life. Forgive me for my past. Take my life and let it shine for You in whatever You've called me to do. Thank You, Lord. In Jesus's name I pray. Amen.*

Maybe you said yes to Jesus at some point in time but have found yourself drifting back to your old life, even if only in your thoughts. If that's the case, now is the perfect time to recommit yourself to that perfect love relationship that sets us free to be all that God has purposed for us. The most important thing to remember about the past—Rebekah's or our own—is not that it was good or evil, but that it is *past*. God has called us out of that past into a relationship and a future with Him. *"Forgetting what is behind and straining toward what is ahead, I press on toward the goal to win the prize for which God has called me heavenward in Christ Jesus"* (Philippians 3:13). Remembering that we have been called to become a part of the bride of Christ, the importance of our role as mothers begins to take on a much nobler light, doesn't it?

## THE PRESENT

Putting the past behind us or focusing on the future isn't nearly as difficult sometimes as living in the present, but that's where we are, isn't it? Today. No more yesterday, not yet tomorrow, but today—and today can be full of challenges. It certainly was for Rebekah.

Rebekah, like her mother-in-law before her, was barren. Despite her beautiful appearance and chaste condition, as well as her willingness to leave her home and family behind to marry Isaac, she could not conceive a child. And that was a source of great grief to her—and to Isaac. Yet Isaac had grown up hearing, again and again, the miraculous story of his own birth—how God had promised Abraham and Sarah a child and, when it was no longer physically possible for them to do so, God intervened and enabled his parents to conceive. So when Rebekah did not get pregnant soon after their marriage, Isaac began to pray for God to open her womb.

Isaac didn't wait to petition God until he and Rebekah had been trying—and failing—for nearly 20 years, though it was that long after their marriage before Esau and Jacob were born. Isaac began to seek God as soon as he realized that his beloved Rebekah was barren. In Genesis 25:21—*"Isaac prayed to the LORD on behalf of his wife, because she was barren"*—the Hebrew word for prayed or entreated, *athar*, may indicate much more than a simple request. The word may denote urging, an ongoing, continual seeking of the Lord about the matter. This was a serious issue for

Isaac and Rebekah, and likely caused much heated and emotional dialog between them, particularly because, until that point in the Scriptures, it seems that men were the only ones to go directly to God. Rebekah, who wanted nothing more at that stage of her life than to be a mother, was anxious to know that her husband was earnestly seeking God on her behalf.

Finally, God answered Isaac's prayer. In fact, He gave them a double blessing—twins! The Scripture says that the twins *"jostled each other within her,"* although jostling doesn't begin to describe what Rebekah was experiencing. This was no ordinary moving about within the womb, as all babies do. The Hebrew word *ratsats,* translated here "jostling," elsewhere carries notions of "to crack in pieces, break, bruise, crush, discourage, oppress, struggle together," It is at this point that we see the first recorded instance of a woman's immediate appeal to God: *"So she went to inquire of the LORD"* (Genesis 25:22).

*Scary to be so vulnerable, isn't it?*

It is worth noting here that, prior to her becoming pregnant, we see no mention of Rebekah's going directly to the Lord. However, once she conceived and began to feel this battle going on inside her, she was driven to her knees to seek God. Why? Because, regardless of our individual situation or circumstance, motherhood changes us. Until a woman feels life inside her womb, everything is about *her.* And then, suddenly, her priorities are rearranged. She wants to know what, when, where, how, why—just like Rebekah. And so, as mothers, we begin to seek God on behalf of our children, even before they are born.

As I mentioned in a previous chapter, there is an old saying that deciding to have a child is like deciding to let your heart walk around outside your body for the rest of your life. As an older woman put it: "When they are young, they're on your knee, but when they're old, they're on your heart." There is a lot of truth in that. Once you are a mother—or a father, for that matter— for as long as you live, wherever your child goes and whatever he does, he takes a big chunk of your heart with him. Scary to be so vulnerable, isn't it? But awesome, too, when you realize that we inherit that pull toward our children from the heavenly Father Himself, the One whose love and longing for us extends far beyond anything we can feel or desire for our own children.

Rebekah's desire to be a mother was fulfilled after 20 long years when her twin boys, Esau and Jacob, were born. Even in birth, as in the womb, the sibling rivalry was evident. Though Esau—whose name denoted thick hair as well as a sense of roughness, a "man's man," if you will—was born first, Jacob was right behind him, grasping his brother's ankle; hence, his name, *Jacob*, which means, "heel-catcher, or supplanter" (meaning, "one who overthrows by tripping up").

The rivalry continued through the years, as the boys' different personalities became more and more evident—and the parents chose sides. Have you ever seen that happen? It's not a pretty sight, and it does nothing but fuel sibling rivalry, as it certainly did in Esau's and Jacob's case. Here were these long-awaited and prayed-for children, each following the bent of his individual personality, at odds with one another and each a pet to one parent.

God's Word instructs us to *"train a child in the way he should go, and when he is old he will not turn from it"* (Proverbs 22:6). Though our first area of direction in this verse is to teach and train our children in the ways of the Scriptures so they will walk in those ways all their lives, there is another implied meaning here. As God is the one who gifts us—and our children—according to His purpose for our lives, it is important for us to recognize and encourage those individual gifts in our children, rather than compare them one to another or try to change them into something God has not called them to be. Sadly, that is what happened with Esau and Jacob.

Esau, the "man's man," loved to hunt and fish and work in the fields. He quickly became his father's favorite, while Jacob, a more thoughtful, introspective, sensitive kind of boy, hung around his mother and easily captured first place in her heart. In fact, we see in Genesis 25:29–34 that Jacob liked to cook. While Esau was out in the *"open country,"* Jacob was at home cooking stew. Esau, famished from his day in the fields, came in and asked his brother for something to eat. Jacob, ever the conniving "heel-catcher," agreed to sell Esau some of his stew in exchange for the birthright that belonged to the eldest son! That's when Esau, short-sighted as he was, made one of the worst trades in the history of the world—the right of the firstborn, which included being the family priest as well as being first in line to inherit all that his father owned, for a bowl of stew.

The sibling rivalry in this family began in the womb and continued into adulthood, causing untold grief to Rebekah and Isaac. And yet these two parents, by playing favorites, added to the problem, rather than solve it. As an immediate result, they missed out on the warmth and unity that should be a normal part of all families who love one another simply because they *are*, rather than for what they do or the personality types they might have.

*They missed out on the warmth and unity that should be a normal part of all families.*

Rebekah had left her past behind and had finally received what she had wanted for so very long—children. Yet things had not turned out as perfectly as she had hoped. Her present was not what she had expected. Though she was undoubtedly pleased that Jacob had managed to usurp Esau's birthright, she also had to realize that the transference of that birthright only deepened the rift between her sons. What she did not *yet* realize was that things would get a lot worse before they got better—and it would cost her more than her mother's heart could even imagine.

## THE FUTURE

Can there be anything worse for a mother than to have a child, whom she has loved and cherished throughout his or her growing-up years, move far away, never to be seen or heard from again? I believe there is. Knowing that she was the cause of that child's departure would make the pain of his absence that much worse. That's what happened to Rebekah, the mother whose dreams for her favorite son, Jacob, moved her to make some foolish choices—and reap some tragic consequences. Let's look at how this situation came to pass.

In biblical times, names meant something. There was a reason for Isaac and Rebekah's sons having the names Esau and Jacob. In truth, there was more than one reason, as is usually the case. The obvious rationale was what their parents saw when their children were born: Esau had lots of thick hair and was, very likely, an aggressive baby, so the name Esau fit him. Jacob, of course, was born holding on to his brother's heel, so "heel-catcher" described him perfectly. But often the names became prophetic, as we see in the lives of these twins as they grew to manhood. Esau was definitely the more physically aggressive of the two, while Jacob was always looking for a way to stop Esau in his tracks and take from him anything of value that he could get his hands on, even if it involved trickery and deception.

> *Rebekah had allowed her love for Jacob to exceed her love for God.*

Where did these boys inherit these characteristics? Esau was an outdoors type, perhaps much like his father, Isaac. Jacob, on the other hand, showed many of his mother's traits—including the use of trickery and deception to get his way. Rebekah— beautiful, chaste virgin that she was when she married Isaac—took first prize when it came to deceit. It wasn't enough for her that Jacob had managed to procure his brother's birthright; she wanted her little darling to have it all—including the lion's share of the patriarchal blessings, which amounted to prophecies for the sons' futures. Rebekah was determined to do whatever it took to see that Jacob got that blessing.

What drove Rebekah to be willing to resort to such devious means? Could it be that, like many mothers, her love for her son sometimes overrode her better judgment? Possibly. However, I believe it was more than that. Rebekah had allowed her love for Jacob to exceed not only her love for her other son, Esau, and even her husband, Isaac, but also her love for God. And that is a very dangerous situation.

Jesus cautioned against this very thing when He said, *"If anyone comes to me and does not hate his father and mother, his wife and children, his brothers and sisters—yes, even his own life—he cannot be my disciple"* (Luke 14:26). Obviously Jesus wasn't saying we had to hate or despise our family members, or even ourselves, in order to be His disciples; what He was saying is that He must come first. In Rebekah's life, that was not the case. The honorable position of motherhood, to which she had been called by God, was dishonored by her misplaced priorities.

Rebekah, out of her inordinate love for her second son, enlisted his help in deceiving Isaac, who felt old and blind, as if he were lying on his deathbed, at the mercy of a family he should have been able to trust. Rebekah had overheard Isaac ask Esau for some of his favorite food as part of the occasion of giving his blessing to his eldest son. Knowing it would take Esau quite a while to hunt, dress, and prepare the game, she intervened by substituting two young goats from the flock and cooking them before Esau could return. She then sent Jacob—disguised as Esau and carrying the food—to fool his father.

Though Isaac was suspicious at first, the deception worked, and the blessing meant for Esau was instead bestowed upon Jacob. When Esau returned with the meat he had hunted and prepared for his father, he learned he was too late. Though he cried and begged his father to bless him as well, Isaac refused to revoke the original blessing. Even though it had been given through trickery, it would not be taken back. There was little left in the way of blessing for Esau.

Needless to say, this escalated the rivalry between the brothers until it became a boiling hatred inside Esau—and a danger to Jacob.

> *Esau held a grudge against Jacob because of the blessing his father had given him. He said to himself, "The days of mourning for my father are near; then I will kill my brother Jacob."*
> —Genesis 27:41

Apparently, though he was talking to himself, he spoke the words out loud because the next verse tells us that when Rebekah found out what Esau had said, she sent for Jacob and told him:

*"Your brother Esau is consoling himself with the thought of killing you. Now then, my son, do what I say: Flee at once to my brother Laban in Haran. Stay with him for a while until your brother's fury subsides. When your brother is no longer angry with you and forgets what you did to him, I'll send word for you to come back from there."*
—Genesis 27: 42–45

Then Rebekah compounded her deceit by lying to Isaac and telling him that she wanted to send Jacob to her brother's family to find a wife, rather than take a chance on his marrying one of the pagan women where they lived. Isaac agreed and *"sent Jacob on his way"* (Genesis 28:5).

*All Rebekah had left was Esau, a son who would always remember.*

How tragic. As a result of Rebekah's deceit, her beloved Jacob was forced to flee for his life. Poor Rebekah surely underestimated the extent of Esau's anger and resentment toward his brother because she told Jacob that once Esau's anger had abated and he forgot what Jacob had done to him, she would send word for him to return. Sadly, Rebekah died before that day ever came. When Isaac *"sent Jacob on his way,"* (Genesis 28:5) it was the last this aging mother ever saw of her favorite son. Instead, she lived out her days with a husband who had lost much of his confidence in her, due to her part in Jacob's deception. Then, once Isaac was dead, all Rebekah had left was Esau, a son who would always remember his mother's part in helping Jacob steal his father's blessing. By the time Jacob returned to the family home 20 years later, Rebekah, too, had died.

And yet, before we condemn Rebekah too harshly, wasn't it God Himself who declared that *"the older will serve the younger"*? Wasn't Rebekah merely "helping" God in assuring that His will and purposes be accomplished?

True, God had indeed declared exactly that, and it was to Rebekah that He had spoken those words. The very fact that

Rebekah had gone to God when she was pregnant shows that she had joined Isaac in his faith in and worship of the true God. The fact that she had believed what God told her about the future of the children in her womb and had begun to think of Jacob as the favored one of God may have affected her own feelings toward both her sons. Where she made her mistake and her faith wavered was when she allowed her attachment to Jacob to supersede her relationship to God and to the other members of her family. As a result, she began to maneuver and manipulate and try to "help" God fulfill His promise, contrary to God's warning and instruction: *"The wise woman builds her house, but with her own hands the foolish one tears hers down"* (Proverbs 14:1).

The wise woman builds; the foolish one tears down. We *build* our house when we build on the foundation of reverential obedience to God and faith in His ability to do what He has promised; we tear it down when we resort to our own resources, regardless of our intentions. Our disobedience and foolishness does not negate God's ability to fulfill His purposes or even to use our actions, nor does it negate the honor and dignity of motherhood. However, it can certainly bring about some tragic consequences.

Can you relate? Have you ever found yourself trying to "help" God, especially when it comes to a situation close to you— particularly if it involves your children? We've all done it, to one degree or another. And we try to convince ourselves that it's OK because, after all, our intentions are good and God's will and purposes are always good, so what could be wrong with a little manipulating to bring His will to pass?

If Rebekah's example isn't warning enough, remember Sarah, Rebekah's mother-in-law. God had promised a child—ultimately Isaac—to Abraham and Sarah, but they were old and nothing was happening. So Sarah decided to help God by giving her maid, Hagar, to Abraham so they could have a child together. From that union came Ishmael—and more trouble than Sarah could ever have imagined. The descendants of Isaac and Ishmael are still fighting to this day, all because Sarah grew impatient and decided to take matters into her own hands.

So, was Rebekah out of God's will when she helped Jacob steal the blessing from Esau? Shouldn't it have been his anyway if he was to rule over his elder brother? Let's answer those questions by posing some others:

- Was God capable and faithful to bring His promise and purpose to pass without Rebekah's deception and manipulation? Absolutely. Deception and manipulation are not of God—ever. These are characteristics that are simply not present in God's character.

- Did God use the situations created by deception and manipulation to accomplish His purposes? Again absolutely. God's plans and purposes are never thwarted because of our weaknesses and sin. God can and will accomplish His purposes, regardless of our choices (see Job 42:2; Romans 8:28). Yet that doesn't necessarily negate the consequences of those choices.

*The last years of Rebekah's life were empty and sad.*

Tragically, the mother who began her life with such purity and innocence ended her days pining away for her beloved son, agonizing to hold him in her arms once more, not living long enough to see him return in triumph with his wives, his children, his flocks and herds and riches. Jacob's future as the father of the 12 tribes of Israel was assured, but the last years of Rebekah's life—which might have been spent with Jacob's children on her lap—were empty and sad. It was a big price to pay, but God's prophetic declaration still came to pass—as it always does, and always will.

*"In God's sovereignty, He will rebuild dreams you hold so close to your heart—dreams for your children and also the dreams you hold for yourself."*
**—Judy Dippel, author**

## Something to Think About/
## Enter in Your Journal:

1. What situations in your life, particularly as a mother, tempt you to try to "help" God fulfill His purposes?

2. If you've given in to those temptations, as most of us have at some time, what were the consequences?

3. What can you do to help ensure that you won't fall into that sort of temptation again?

*"Every mother is like Moses. She does not enter the promised land. She prepares a world she will not see."*
—**Pope Paul VI**

# A Mother's Prayer

*Dear Lord, help me always to keep in mind that it is Your promises and Your purposes that must be fulfilled, not mine—and that they will best be fulfilled in Your way and Your time. Seal that to my heart, Father, and help me to walk in the honor of motherhood and appreciation for the blessing of children. In Jesus's name. Amen.*

**"A mother's love transcends all space and time."**
**—Dayle Shockley**

*"Positive results are manifested through mothers persevering in prayer."*

—Jean Whitlow, mother, grandmother, minister

# CHAPTER 4

# Rachel and Leah: Competing Through Their Children

*Now Laban had two daughters: the name of the elder was Leah, and the name of the younger was Rachel. . . . Now Jacob loved Rachel.*
—Genesis 29:16, 18

SUGGESTED SCRIPTURE READINGS:
Genesis 29–33; 35:16–19; 46:15–18; Ruth 4:11; Jeremiah 31:15; Matthew 2:18

Have you noticed that all families, including our own, have certain traits—some good, some... well, not so good? This has always been so, including in the family and descendants of the great patriarch Abraham.

Remember Abraham's wife, Sarah, and the ongoing competition she had with Hagar after Ishmael was born, long before Isaac was conceived? And then there was the competition between Isaac and Rebekah's twins, Esau and Jacob, much of which was instigated or at least heightened by Rebekah's favoritism toward Jacob.

In this next generation of Abraham and Sarah's family, we find a level of competition between Rachel and Leah that can only be found between two sisters, both married to the same man. If you've ever been in competition with a sister—or a friend, or maybe even your husband's former spouse—you'll find this chapter of particular interest.

❖ ❖ ❖

Though the Scriptures don't specifically tell us, it is easy to assume that Rachel and Leah lived in a level of competition long before Jacob entered the fray. Leah was the older daughter, a position that carried certain responsibilities and privileges, not the least of which was the presumed right to marry ahead of any younger sisters. Rachel, on the other hand, was the more beautiful of the two, a fact that undoubtedly had not been lost on either of them.

We can only imagine there were other suitors before Jacob, who were introduced to and encouraged to pursue Leah, even while their attention was drawn to Rachel. But from the time Jacob first laid eyes on the lovely young shepherdess named Rachel, the scene was set for a competitive clash that would pit sister against sister, wife against husband, daughter against father—and, ultimately, brother against brother.

Jacob, of course, knew none of this when he first arrived in the low-lying hillside near the city of Haran in Padan-aram, more than 500 miles from his home in what is now known as Palestine. He was simply a man on a mission—namely, to escape the wrath of his brother, Esau, whom he had deceived (with the help of his mother, Rebekah)—with the secondary mission of finding a wife among his mother's relatives. Little did Jacob know that he, the trickster and deceiver of his brother, was himself about to be deceived in such a way that would deeply affect his descendants for generations to come.

In the culture of Jacob's day, it was not unusual for people to be much more demonstrative than we of Western culture today. It was not surprising, therefore, that after a journey of more than 500 miles, Jacob was excited and emotional when he came upon one of his mother's relatives—and it certainly didn't hurt that she was young and beautiful.

The Bible tells us that when Jacob saw Rachel and was told that she was the daughter of his mother's brother Laban, he went to her and gave her a kiss of greeting, and then *"lifted up his voice and wept"* (Genesis 29:11). When he then explained to her that he was Rebekah's son, the equally emotional and excitable Rachel ran to her father and told him the news.

By that time, of course, Jacob was already smitten. When Laban arrived to welcome him and take him to his home, we are told that *Jacob "stayed with him [Laban] for a month"* (Genesis 29:14).

*Seven years' wages was no small amount.*

It's a safe assumption that during that time Jacob earned his keep by helping Laban because in verse 15 Laban said to Jacob, *"Because you are my relative, should you therefore serve me for nothing? Tell me, what should your wages be?"*

Here we have the first inkling of how deep Jacob's feelings ran for Rachel, when he answered, *"I will serve you seven years for Rachel your younger daughter"* (Genesis 29:18).

Seven years' wages was no small amount; in fact, it was considerably more than the going bride-price of the day—and crafty Uncle Laban knew that. He also knew he had an older daughter, Leah, with *"delicate"* eyes (Genesis 29:17), whom he fully intended to marry off before parting with Rachel. Of course, he conveniently ignored that fact when he answered Jacob by saying, *"It is better that I give her to you than that I should give her to another man. Stay with me"* (Genesis 29:19).

And so Jacob entered into a seven-year agreement with Laban, fully expecting that at the end of that seven-year period he would receive his beloved Rachel as his wife. In fact, verse 20 shows us how intense was Jacob's love for Rachel: *"So Jacob served seven years for Rachel, and they seemed but a few days to him because of the love he had for her."*

At the end of those seven years, during which Laban benefited greatly from Jacob's conscientious work, Jacob said to his uncle, *"Give me my wife, for my days are fulfilled, that I may go in to her"* (Genesis 29:21).

At last! More than seven years after Jacob had first been captivated by the sight of the beautiful young shepherdess named Rachel, he was about to take her as his wife—or so he had been led to believe. But Laban had a very big trick up his sleeve. When the wedding feast was ended and it was time for Jacob to go to his new wife and consummate their marriage, Laban substituted Leah for Rachel. Due to the custom of the day, which amounted to the bride being led to her husband under cover of night, this was not so difficult as we might think—so long as neither Rachel nor Leah blew the whistle on their sly old dad.

We can only wonder, of course, at Rachel's motives for not saying anything. Was she unaware of the switch until it was too late? Was she commanded to remain silent by her father to whom she still owed her allegiance? Is it possible she didn't return Jacob's feelings for her? Doubtful, since we later see her competing fiercely with her sister for Jacob's attentions. Whatever the reason, Rachel said nothing, and Laban's "bait-and-switch" tactics worked, for the next morning Jacob woke up to find himself sleeping next to the "delicate-eyed" Leah, rather than the breathtakingly beautiful Rachel—and he was not a happy camper.

*"What is this you have done to me?"* Jacob asked in verse 25. *"Was it not for Rachel that I served you? Why then have you deceived me?"*

Laban's answer was as forthcoming as it was logical—for their day and time—and it left Jacob with little alternative if he still wanted Rachel for his wife.

*"It must not be done so in our country, to give the younger before the firstborn,"* Laban explained. *"Fulfill her week, and we*

*will give you this one also for the service which you will serve with me still another seven years"* (Genesis 29:27).

Notice the brevity of Laban's recorded explanation. There was a reason for that, namely that he realized he wasn't telling Jacob anything he didn't already know. Jacob, however, had hoped to circumvent this well-known cultural tradition of the oldest daughter being married first through the agreement he had made with Laban, but it was not to be. Leah became Jacob's wife because she was Laban's oldest daughter. Then, if Jacob was willing to work for Laban for another seven years, he could have Rachel too. That was the deal, take it or leave it.

He took it—and the rest, as they say, is history. According to verse 28, Jacob *"fulfilled"* Leah's week, giving her the attention a new bride deserved, and then he took Rachel to be his second wife—the wife of his heart—and Leah was quickly relegated to second place. The triangle was established, and as Jacob worked to complete his second seven-year stint, the competition heated up to unimagined levels.

## LEAH

We speculated on why Rachel didn't say anything about her father's deception of Jacob, but why was Leah silent? Was she attracted to Jacob, wanting him for herself? Was she tired of Rachel getting all the attention, while she languished in the background? Was she determined to obey her father and fulfill the cultural tradition of being married before her sister? Was she afraid that Jacob might be her only chance at finding a husband?

*And that fueled the fire for some seriously stiff competition.*

Possibly the answer is yes—to all of the above. Again, we don't really know Leah's motivations, but the possibilities are numerous. Whatever the reason, she went along with her father's deception and gained a husband—at least, in name. But did she ever own his heart? To the degree that Rachel did, probably not, though that certainly doesn't mean she didn't try. And that fueled the fire for some seriously stiff competition.

So where was God in all this? He was exactly where He always is—deeply involved in every aspect of our lives, caring for us and working things together to achieve His purposes, even when the circumstances are other than what He might want for us.

Certainly God is not a God who advocates deception—and yet He can still use the circumstances produced by deception to fulfill His plans. And that's what happened in the case of Jacob and his two wives.

Verse 30 tells us that Jacob *"loved Rachel more than Leah,"* and even if Jacob made a concerted effort not to make his preference obvious, Leah was no fool. She may have been silent about her father's deception of Jacob, but she was certainly privy to it. She knew she was gaining a husband by default, and that can't do much for a lady's confidence. After the first week of Leah's marriage, during which Jacob "fulfilled" his duty to her, the poor girl had to notice how cold and lonely her bed was when her husband beat a hasty retreat from her bedroom to Rachel's. It can't have been an easy adjustment, and "primary wife" or not, Leah knew she was not Jacob's first choice.

That's when God stepped in—as He always does, right on time. Verse 31 says, *"When the LORD saw that Leah was unloved, He opened her womb; but Rachel was barren."* This was no small deal in a culture and time when barren women were considered cursed and men counted their blessings by how many sons they had. How Leah's heart must have swelled with joy and hope, even as her abdomen swelled with her growing child. The next verses seem to confirm that thought.

> *So Leah conceived and bore a son, and she called his name Reuben; for she said, "The LORD has surely looked on my affliction. Now therefore, my husband will love me." Then she conceived again and bore a son, and said, "Because the LORD has heard that I am unloved, He has therefore given me this son also." And she called his name Simeon. She conceived again and bore a son, and said, "Now this time my husband will become attached to me, because I have borne him three sons." Therefore his name*

*was called Levi. And she conceived again and bore a son, and said, "Now I will praise the LORD. "Therefore she called his name Judah. Then she stopped bearing.*
—Genesis 29:32–35

From the names Leah bestowed on her sons, it is easy to see that with the birth of each of her first three sons, she hoped she would gain her husband's love. By the birth of her fourth son, Judah, her focus has moved from her husband to God. Is it possible that by that time she had given up trying to win her husband's love and had learned to find her fulfillment in a love relationship with God? Again, we are speculating, but it might certainly seem to be so.

Delicate-eyed Leah, the elder but less attractive sister, had borne her husband four sons, while Rachel, the more beautiful and beloved sister, had given him none. What animosity and jealousy must have marked the relationship of these two sisters who shared the same husband—and what drama lay ahead for this complex and ever-growing family.

## TO THE NEXT GENERATION

Jacob's children didn't stop with the birth of Leah's four sons. In Genesis 30 we see that Rachel has begun to blame Jacob for not impregnating her, though it doubtless wasn't because he didn't try. When Rachel stormed at him and cried, *"Give me children, or else I die!"* (Genesis 30:1), the poor man became angry with the woman he loved and replied, *"Am I in the place of God, who has withheld from you the fruit of the womb?"* (Genesis 30:2).

He was right, of course. Jacob could perform the physical act that preceded pregnancy, but he could not ensure the conception of a child. Only God could open or close a womb, and so Rachel's demands were pointless. Realizing that, she resorted to the custom of the day and gave her maid, Bilhah, to Jacob, telling him, *"Go in to her, and she will bear a child on my knees, that I also may have children by her"* (Genesis 30:3). Jacob listened to his wife, and soon Bilhah had a child by Jacob, and Rachel named him Dan, saying,

"God has judged my case; and He has also heard my voice and given me a son" (Genesis 30:6). Bilhah soon conceived again and bore another son, whom Rachel named Naphtali because she said, *"With great wrestlings I have wrestled with my sister, and indeed I have prevailed"* (Genesis 30:8).

*She also wanted to outdo her sister.*

Not only did Rachel want sons to present to her husband, but she also wanted to outdo her sister. The competition continued—"wrestlings," according to Rachel—and Jacob was caught right in the middle of it.

By this time Leah realized she wasn't getting pregnant again, and so she too gave her maid to Jacob, who now had two wives and two concubines. Leah's maid, Zilpah, conceived and bore a son whom Leah named "Gad," meaning *"a troop comes"* (Genesis 30:11), and then another son, whom Leah named Asher, meaning *"I am happy, for the daughters will call me blessed"* (Genesis 30:13). Jacob's family was growing by leaps and bounds.

Then one day Leah's son Reuben found some mandrakes, a fruit that was believed to enhance fertility and improve the chances of conception. When Rachel saw the mandrakes, she asked Leah for some, but Leah wasn't feeling very generous toward her little sister.

*"Is it a small matter that you have taken away my husband?"* Leah asked. *"Would you take away my son's mandrakes also?"* (Genesis 30:15).

You can almost see Rachel's pout when she answers, *"Therefore he will lie with you tonight for your son's mandrakes"* (Genesis 30:15).

Whether or not the mandrakes had any effect, verse 16 tells us that Jacob slept with Leah that night. Verse 17 then tells us that *"God listened to Leah, and she conceived and bore Jacob a fifth son"* (Genesis 30:17). This son she named Issachar, saying *"God has given me my hire, because I have given my maid to my husband"* (Genesis 30:18). Soon after Leah conceived again and bore yet another son, this one named Zebulun, and she declared,

*"God has endowed me with a good endowment; now my husband will dwell with me, because I have borne him six sons"* (Genesis 30:20). Verse 21 then tells us that Leah conceived and bore a daughter and named her Dinah.

Then, in verse 22, we once again see God stepping in to fulfill a heart's desire and to accomplish His own purpose:

> *Then God remembered Rachel, and God listened to her and opened her womb. And she conceived and bore a son, and said, "God has taken away my reproach." So she called his name Joseph, and said, "The LORD shall add to me another son."*
> —Genesis 30:22–24

Not only did Rachel finally bear a son, but she made the prophetic declaration that she would bear another. Had the fact that God had "remembered" her and given her a son also birthed a faith in her that enabled her to believe in another yet to come? More speculation, but certainly a possibility.

By this time Jacob had lived with Laban for about 20 years, and he was longing to go home. According to the laws of his time, however, this would not be an easy break, since Laban could claim not only his children, meaning Rachel and Leah, as his own, but his grandchildren as well. So Jacob began to plot and plan and scheme—something both he and Laban were quite adept at doing—to find a way to take his family and his belongings and return to the land of Abraham and Sarah, Isaac and Rebekah.

Now, for the first time, we see Rachel and Leah united in purpose. For whatever reason, they too wanted to leave their father and return with Jacob to his home, and so they worked together with their husband, counseling and advising him, in order to make their dream become a reality.

It is indeed amazing to see people who have long been at odds suddenly come together in common purpose, and here is a clear picture of such an occurrence in Genesis 31, where Rachel and Leah speak to Jacob in unison, saying,

*"Is there still any portion or inheritance for us in our father's house? Are we not considered strangers by him? For he has sold us, and also completely consumed our money. For all these riches which God has taken from our father are really ours and our children's; now then, whatever God has said to you, do it."*
—Genesis 31:14–16

It seems the daughters weren't too happy with the fact that their father was appropriating the wealth that had come to them because of their husband's hard work, and so they were more than willing to pack up their children and their belongings and head for greener pastures. And so, according to verse 17,

*Jacob rose and set his sons and his wives on camels. And he carried away all his livestock and all his possessions which he had gained, his acquired livestock which he had gained in Padan Aram, to go to his father Isaac in the land of Canaan.*

We know, of course, that Isaac and Rebekah were already dead by this time. Still, Esau was the only one left of the family Jacob had left behind, and Jacob had no idea what sort of welcome to expect from the brother he had deceived so many years earlier.

*Jacob had no idea what sort of welcome to expect.*

Here again we see Jacob's preferential treatment of Rachel over Leah. Hoping for the best but anticipating the worst, Jacob arranged his family by priority. Genesis 33:2 tells us that when he saw his brother, Esau, coming toward him, *"he put the maidservants and their children in front, Leah and her children behind, and Rachel and Joseph last."* Then *"he crossed over before them and bowed himself to the ground seven times, until he came near to his brother"* (Genesis 33:3), hoping to gain his brother's favor and preserve all of his family alive.

Apparently the 20 years had mellowed Esau and dulled the sharpness of his memory of Jacob's deception because *"Esau ran to meet him [Jacob], and embraced him, and fell on his neck and kissed him, and they wept"* (Genesis 33:4). The brothers were reunited, and Jacob's wives, concubines, children, and servants continued their journey in safety.

And yet, isn't it logical to assume that Leah understood why she was put just behind the maidservants and their children but in front of Rachel and Joseph? The assigned order was clear: Leah was more important to Jacob than his concubines, but she had still not gained an equal place in his heart with Rachel. The joy of being safely welcomed to their new home by Esau must have been severely dampened by the reminder that she would never be the preferred and most loved wife. She would live in her younger sister's shadow for the rest of their days.

*Give me children, or else I die!*

And then Rachel's prophetic proclamation that she would one day bear another child came to pass. Genesis 35:16–20 tells the story this way:

> *Rachel labored in childbirth, and she had hard labor. Now it came to pass, when she was in hard labor, that the midwife said to her, "Do not fear; you will have this son also." And so it was, as her soul was departing (for she died), that she called his name Ben-Oni; but his father called him Benjamin. So Rachel died and was buried on the way to Ephrath (that is, Bethlehem). And Jacob set a pillar on her grave, which is the pillar of Rachel's grave to this day.*

Jacob's beloved wife, Rachel, was dead, leaving behind a son she named "Ben-Oni," son of sorrow, but whose name was changed to *Benjamin*, son of his right hand, by his father. Did Rachel's words, *"Give me children, or else I die!"* (Genesis 30:1) echo in Jacob's ears as he said goodbye to his beloved? His own, more recent words, may also have haunted him, for when he took his family and fled from Laban, he was unaware that Rachel had stolen her father's household gods. When Laban tracked them down and demanded the idols be returned, Jacob had replied, *"With whomever you find your gods, do not let him live"* (Genesis 31:32). Though Laban did not find the idols, since Rachel had positioned herself to cover them, Jacob's pronouncement still came to pass.

And so, this man who had worked 14 years to gain the woman he loved now buried her "on the way to Ephrath" and erected a pillar to mark the spot. And Leah finally had her husband to herself.

Did Jacob then turn to Leah at long last, devoting himself to her and giving her the love and attention she had desired for so many years? The Scriptures don't really tell us that, though there is an interesting point that may indicate that they at least became quite close in their latter years.

In the meantime, however, the competition between Rachel and Leah extended to their sons, so much so that the sons of Leah and the concubines conspired to kill Joseph, Jacob's favorite. Though Joseph wasn't killed, he was sold into slavery, even spending time in prison in Egypt. And yet God used those tragic circumstances as well, eventually elevating Joseph to second-in-command in Egypt and enabling many people, including Jacob and his entire family, to be preserved from the famine that killed so many others.

In the end, however, we note the point that implies the closeness that may finally have developed between Jacob and Leah. If nothing else, it certainly proves that Jacob honored Leah's position as the first or primary wife, for when we read of Jacob's death in the land of Egypt, we see that he made his son Joseph promise to bury him with his "fathers," meaning Abraham and Sarah, Isaac and Rebekah—and Leah (Genesis 47:27–31). Jacob, or Israel as he was called by that time, didn't request that Joseph transport Rachel's bones to be buried in the family plot or tomb, but rather that Joseph carry Jacob's bones out of Egypt to be buried with his "fathers"—and with Leah, the wife he had been tricked into marrying when all he wanted was her younger sister, Rachel.

Delicate-eyed Leah, the unloved and unfavored wife, would finally have preeminence over Rachel, the beautiful and favorite one. At last Leah would lie beside her husband in the place of honor that she had missed throughout the years of her marriage.

As for the family rivalry, beginning with Rachel and Leah and then cultivated and perpetuated by Laban and his trickery and eventually extended to Isaac's sons, how did it finally end? The sons were at last reconciled, though it took place in the courts of Egypt, where Joseph had risen to a position of glory and power. At last the brothers were able to put away the sibling rivalry that had haunted their mothers and put great stress on their father. Thanks to Joseph, Rachel's firstborn, the rest of Jacob's children and their families were fed and cared for throughout the famine that plagued the land. The family was at last united, and Jacob, Rachel, and Leah no doubt rested in peace, as God faithfully fulfilled His promise and purpose to the patriarchs of His chosen people, Israel.

*"The most important thing a father can do for his children is to love their mother."*
—**Theodore Hesburgh, activist**

## Something to Think About/
## Enter in Your Journal:

1. What long-standing issue in your life has caused a sense of rivalry in your family, whether between yourself and someone else, or other family members?

2. How can your understanding of the story of Rachel and Leah help you be a part of bringing a peaceful resolution to that long-standing rivalry?

3. Explain what you see as the outcomes that could occur in your family's future generations if the rivalry is or is not resolved.

*"The tie which links mother and child is of such pure and immaculate strength as to never be violated."*
**—Washington Irving, author, historian**

## A Mother's Prayer

*Father, thank You that even in the midst of circumstances that are not pleasing to You, You can still accomplish Your purposes for our lives. Please help me see how You want me to be an instrument of peace and reconciliation in these situations. In Jesus's name. Amen.*

**"One of God's richest blessings is that our children come into the world as people we're supposed to guide and direct, and then God uses them to form us— if we'll only listen."**
**—Dena Dyer, author**

"*The formative period of building character for eternity is in the nursery; the mother is queen of that realm and sways a scepter more potent than that of kings or priests.*"

—Author unknown

# CHAPTER 5

# Jochebed: The Greatest Sacrifice

*When she* [Jochebed] *saw that he* [Moses] was *a beautiful* child, *she hid him three months. But when she could no longer hide him, she took an ark of bulrushes... put the child in it, and laid* it *in the reeds by the river's bank.*
—Exodus 2:2–3

SUGGESTED SCRIPTURE READINGS:
Exodus 2:1–10; 6:20; Numbers 26:59

Jochebed was a woman characterized by courageous, self-sacrificing love. In today's "it's all about me" society, those qualities are precious and rare. Yet was it so different in Jochebed's time? Life certainly wasn't easy then, especially for the Hebrews who had become slaves in the land of Egypt.

Every day was a struggle just to survive, and fear had become a constant companion. After all, what could be more terrifying than for a Hebrew mother to hear the edict that all males born to the Hebrews must die?

This Hebrew mother considered her son "beautiful," meaning he was precious in her sight. And isn't that exactly how each of us mothers feels about our children, particularly when we first lay eyes on them after they're born? Imagine how we would feel if, upon seeing that our newborn was a male, we realized he was marked for murder. How far would we be willing to go to protect and deliver that innocent baby from death?

❖ ❖ ❖

Jochebed was the mother of the famous Hebrew deliverer and lawgiver, Moses, as well as Moses's older brother, Aaron, and sister, Miriam. Like her husband, Amram, Jochebed was of the tribe of Levi, the tribe from which the priests of Israel descended. Jochebed was a godly woman, and she and her husband trained their older son, Aaron, who would become the center and founder of the Hebrew priesthood, in which he served for almost 40 years. Miriam, too, grew up to be a leader of the Hebrew people. But it was Moses whose personal destiny would influence and help fulfill that of the entire nation of God's chosen people.

As we begin the study of this faithful mother, it is important to note that though Moses was born at what most would consider an inopportune time in history, he still rose to great heights and is remembered today as one of the greatest men who ever lived. He accomplished this against all odds. Why? Because God is faithful and had a purpose for Moses's life, of course—but also because Moses had a mother who was not afraid to do what was right, even when it meant putting herself in possible danger by defying the authorities, as well as suffering great personal loss by giving up her beloved son to be raised by someone else. It was a great price to pay, but the reward was the deliverance of Israel from captivity and slavery.

Can there be anything more heartrending than a mother giving up her own child, even though she knows she's doing it for the child's best interests? How many stories through the ages have we heard of a mother who had to make such a painful choice in order to save her child's life? And yet, out of pure and selfless love, that choice was made. Who knows how many destinies have been changed as a result?

Of course, such choices aren't always quite as dramatic as Jochebed's, where she had to hide her baby boy in a basket so he wouldn't be murdered by Pharaoh's henchmen. In our society, this type of selfless mother-love is best illustrated by the woman who, for whatever reason, finds herself in a position where she can't adequately care for her child, and so she gives up her parental rights and allows the baby to be adopted and raised by someone else. This is not an easy decision for any mother, regardless of her circumstances, and she is to be commended for putting the child's welfare above her own and for not giving in to the quick and easy "solution" offered by the world today—abortion. Mothers who place their little ones for adoption are choosing to give their babies physical life, as well as the chance to grow up and fulfill the destiny and purpose God has for them.

Jochebed was such a woman. With two children to care for already, she bore her third child—a son—right in the midst of the time that the current Pharaoh was hard at work trying to maintain control over the Hebrew slaves by having their baby boys thrown into the Nile and drowned. His reasoning was that the slave nation was growing too quickly, and he feared that they would become so strong they would rise up in rebellion and defeat their captors. At first he ordered the Hebrew midwives to do his dirty work and kill the baby boys as soon as they were born. What he didn't understand was that the midwives feared God more than they feared Pharaoh, and so they did the right thing and let the babies live, telling Pharaoh that the Hebrew women gave birth quickly and didn't give the midwives time to get there to assist in the births.

Pharaoh then ordered his own assassins to hunt down these baby boys and throw them into a watery grave. How many nights did Jochebed lie awake, listening to the weeping and wailing of Hebrew mothers whose babies had been killed and wondering when the murderers would come for her own newborn? How many times did she pray that God would help her hide her precious son and preserve his life?

But after three months, the Bible tells us, Jochebed could no longer hide her baby. For whatever reason, she realized she had to take drastic action if she wanted to give her son a chance to grow up. If that meant giving him up and breaking her own heart in the process, so be it.

*She realized she had to take drastic action.*

And so we read in Exodus 2:3, *"She took an ark of bulrushes for him, daubed it with asphalt and pitch, put the child in it, and laid it in the reeds by the river's bank."* Jochebed then instructed her daughter, Miriam, to stand watch over her little brother—far enough away that she wouldn't be seen, but close enough to know what would become of the baby in the basket.

What an incredibly difficult time that must have been, both for Jochebed as she awaited word from her daughter, and for Miriam as she watched and waited. Where was Amram while this was going on? The Scriptures don't tell us, but if he was an able-bodied man, he was undoubtedly away from home, slaving away in one capacity or another for Pharaoh. Whether or not he was even aware of the heartache going on in his family or the drama going on at the river is unknown. However, there is no doubt that he heard all about it when he returned home at the end of a long day.

## RAISING HIM UP

That God would use Pharaoh's own daughter to rescue this baby boy is in itself a miraculous occurrence. Who better to assure the young child's safety than Pharaoh's daughter?

As Miriam waited and watched near the river, Jochebed waited and prayed at home. Is there any doubt she cried out to God from the depths of a broken heart, as tears streamed down her face and her full breasts ached to give nourishment to the wee one whose hungry cry they could no longer satisfy?

Yet, as Miriam watched and Jochebed prayed, the Scriptures tell us that *"the daughter of Pharaoh came down to wash herself at the river"* (Exodus 2:5). Her maids were with her, and when she saw the "ark," or basket, floating among the reeds by the river's edge, she sent one of her maids to get it. Then, the Bible tells us, she opened it and looked inside, and *"the baby wept"* (Exodus 2:6). What woman can resist a crying baby, especially one floating in a basket on the river? Apparently Pharaoh's daughter's heart wasn't as hard as her father's, for when she saw the baby and heard him cry, *"she had compassion on him"* (Exodus 2:6). She immediately recognized that he was one of the Hebrew babies and that someone—probably his mother—had placed him in the basket in hopes that he would be rescued and delivered from the death decree that swept the land.

And so she did just that. Even as Pharaoh's daughter looked with compassion on this obviously distressed infant, young Miriam approached and asked, *"Shall I go and call a nurse for you from the Hebrew women, that she may nurse the child for you?"* (Exodus 2:7). This was a natural question, since it was obvious that Pharaoh's daughter couldn't nurse the baby. In addition, wet nurses were common in those days, and still are in some cultures today. God had placed not only Pharaoh's daughter in the right place at the right time to effect Moses's deliverance, but He had placed Miriam there as well. The girl asked the right question at the right time, and Pharaoh's daughter readily agreed.

> God had answered a mother's prayers.

Can you imagine the joy and relief that washed over Jochebed when Miriam returned with the news? "Come, Mother," she may have said. "Pharaoh's daughter herself has rescued our baby, and she needs you to nurse him for her." My Lord!

God had answered a mother's prayers for protection and deliverance for her child, and He had given her a bonus as only God could: She would now get to hold her baby at her breast and nourish him under the safety and protection of Pharaoh's daughter.

It must have seemed almost too good to be true.

But true it was. When Jochebed and Miriam hurried back to Pharaoh's daughter, it required all the restraint this joyous mother had not to immediately snatch up her little son and clutch him to her heart. Undoubtedly, however, she humbly and submissively approached this royal rescuer of her child and awaited instruction.

*"Take this child away and nurse him for me, and I will give you your wages,"* Pharaoh's daughter told her (Exodus 2:9). Jochebed's hands must have shook as she took her baby back into her arms, marveling that she would not only get to help raise her son without fear of Pharaoh's murderous edict invading their home, but she was to be paid for doing so!

Verse 10 of this same chapter tells us how this relationship progressed: *"And the child grew, and she* [Jochebed] *brought him to Pharaoh's daughter, and he became her son. So she called his name Moses, saying, 'Because I drew him out of the water.'"* So it was actually Pharaoh's daughter who gave Moses his name. Did he have a Hebrew name before that? If so, it isn't mentioned in the Scriptures. It is mentioned, however, that though Jochebed had the joy and privilege of nursing her son and watching him grow, it was Pharaoh's daughter who was considered his mother.

Was that difficult for Jochebed? I'm sure it was, especially once the boy was weaned and there was no more excuse for this dear mother to continue to hold her child and enjoy that amazing bond that only a nursing mother and baby can share. And yet, throughout that time, while Jochebed reveled in the feel of her son's soft skin and the sweet smell of his presence, there is little doubt she prayed for him, sang to him, whispered her undying love to him. Was Moses old enough to remember any of that? We don't know that either, but God remembered—and He honored every word this selfless mother prayed on her son's behalf.

# HOLDING HIM UP

So what happened to Jochebed's role as mother once Moses was weaned and her service as wet nurse was no longer needed? Again, we have nothing in the Scriptures to clarify this point, but we can only imagine that like any other mother, her heart continued to long for her child. No doubt Jochebed took every possible opportunity to watch her son from afar. How she must have ached to run to him and throw her arms around him and say, "Moses, I'm your mother! Me, Jochebed—not Pharaoh's daughter!" But, of course, she couldn't. To fulfill the longing in her own heart would have been to put her beloved son in danger. And so she kept her pain inside, possibly sharing it with Amram when they lay in each other's arms at night, or with Miriam when they shared the household chores during the day. And no doubt she poured out her heart to the Lord—all day, every day, with each waking moment.

"Care for him, LORD," she would pray while cooking what little food they had.

"Protect him, God," she begged as she drifted off at night.

"Keep him close, LORD," she implored if she happened to catch a glimpse of him during the course of the day.

Moses no doubt knew he was not the natural son of Pharaoh's daughter; in fact, his adopted mother may even have told him the story of how he was rescued from the river and named Moses.

*It didn't stop her from talking to the God of Israel.*

He may even have had a suspicion that the woman named Jochebed, who had nursed him when he was young, was his natural mother, but it's doubtful he knew that as a fact, since it would have been far too dangerous for Jochebed and her family—and possibly even for Moses—for this news to become common knowledge. For that reason, Jochebed continued to keep her family's secret locked in her aching heart.

But it didn't stop her from talking to the God of Israel, the One who had promised Abraham, Isaac, and Jacob that He would make a great nation from them, the God who promised through Joseph that this great nation would one day be delivered from

Egypt. And so, throughout Moses's life, during each stage of his development, Jochebed prayed for him. Though she had no direct contact with him, she followed his life as best she could, knowing he was becoming a man and praying for the fulfillment of God's purpose for his life.

Isn't that what we all do as mothers? Whether our children are preschoolers or teenagers or adults with families of their own; whether they are preachers or politicians or bus drivers, we need to pray for the fulfillment of God's purpose in their lives, even as Jochebed did in the land of Egypt. But we must also remember that at times, even as we are faithful to pray, we may experience some startling, and even terrifying, events.

How must Jochebed have felt when she heard the news that Moses, by then a grown man, had killed an Egyptian in defense of a Hebrew slave? No doubt she heard of it, and it must have struck terror into her heart. Exodus 2:11–12 describes the event this way:

> *Now it came to pass in those days, when Moses was grown, that he went out to his brethren and looked at their burdens. And he saw an Egyptian beating a Hebrew, one of his brethren. So he looked this way and that way, and when he saw no one, he killed the Egyptian and hid him in the sand.*

These two verses make it clear that Moses evidently knew that he was a Hebrew by birth. His reaction to seeing *"one of his brethren"* being beaten by an Egyptian—even though Moses himself was being raised as an Egyptian—caused an immediate reaction, one that would have a major impact on his life and destiny. As we see in the next two verses, this violent act on Moses's part quickly became known among the Hebrews. Moses realized then that it was only a matter of time until the news reached Pharaoh's ears, and even Moses's adopted mother wouldn't be able to help him then.

Moses was right, of course. Verse 15 tells us, *"When Pharaoh heard of this matter, he sought to kill Moses. But Moses fled from the face of Pharaoh and dwelt in the land of Midian."* Moses, born to Hebrew slaves, threatened with death while still a baby, hidden in a basket on the Nile, then rescued from his hiding place and raised in royalty, was now on the run, his life once again in danger. Had all of Jochebed's self-sacrifice been for nothing? Was her beloved Moses going to die at the hands of Pharaoh after all? Was Jochebed even still alive when this event took place?

This latter is another question for which we have no answer. However, even if Jochebed was no longer on this earth, praying for her son's protection, God had long before heard her prayers, and even before Jochebed uttered her first intercession for her son, God had determined Moses's destiny. God is not limited by time or place or circumstances. Pharaoh might be breathing fire at Moses, determined to kill the man he no doubt considered an ungrateful Hebrew slave who had turned on his adopted people, the Egyptians...but God had other plans. And God's plans always come to pass, just as they would for Moses in the land of Midian.

> *Before Jochebed uttered her first intercession for her son, God had determined Moses's destiny.*

When Moses arrived in this desert land, verse 15 tells us *"he sat down by a well."* Undoubtedly tired and thirsty, he first took a drink of cool water before taking a much-needed rest and trying to decide what to do next. Did he offer a prayer during that time? The Scriptures don't mention it, but chances are that he did. If he knew he was a Hebrew, then he knew about the Hebrew God. It's possible he may even have remembered some of the things Jochebed told him about that God when he was a very young boy, nursing at his mother's breast, as children weren't weaned in those days nearly as early as they are now.

But whether Moses prayed or not as he sat there at the well, God saw him and sent seven sisters to escort him on the next leg of his journey. These seven sisters were the daughters of Reuel, the priest of Midian, and they came to the well to draw water for themselves and for their father's flock. We then read in verse 17 that *"the shepherds came and drove them [the seven daughters of Reuel] away; but Moses stood up and helped them, and watered their flock."* When the sisters went home and told their fathers how a stranger had helped them, he immediately told them to go bring the man home for a meal. And what a meal it must have been! For immediately following Reuel's invitation for Moses to eat with them in verse 20, we see in the very next verse that things seemed to progress well and quickly: *"Then Moses was content to live with the man, and he gave Zipporah his daughter to Moses"* (Exodus 2:21).

In the matter of a few verses—and probably in a relatively short period of time—Moses went from homeless fugitive to son-in-law of the priest of Midian. Though Jochebed, if she was indeed still alive when this event took place, didn't know what was transpiring in her son's life, God had made a way for the fulfillment of Moses's destiny to move to the next step.

> *Though Jochebed didn't know what was transpiring in her son's life, God had made a way.*

Did everything fall into place quickly after that? Not at all. If Moses's destiny included being used by God to deliver the Hebrew nation from slavery in Egypt, you'd think it would happen in much the same rapid manner as his ousting from Egypt and relocating in Midian. But that isn't how it took place at all. In fact, Moses spent the next 40 years of his life as a shepherd in the desert, undoubtedly relearning a lot of what he had been taught while growing up in a pagan palace.

Life may not have been easy for Moses during that time in the desert, particularly since he had been accustomed to the luxuries of wealth and privilege in Pharaoh's court. But the life he led in Midian was still a vast improvement over the living conditions of his Hebrew kinsmen back in Egypt who, according to Exodus 2:23, *"cried out"* to God over the ever-increasing bondage put on them by their Egyptian taskmasters. The next verses go on to assure us that

> *Their* [the Hebrews'] *cry came up to God because of the bondage. So God heard their groaning, and God remembered His covenant with Abraham, with Isaac, and*

*with Jacob. And God looked upon the children of Israel,
and God acknowledged them.*
—Exodus 2:23–25

Now it was time for God to act, time for Moses once again to move
into the next leg of the journey, the next season of his destiny. It
was there that the Angel of the Lord called to him from within a
flame of fire in a bush—and Moses turned aside to see why the
bush wasn't consumed.

Notice Moses didn't respond in immediate reverence and
obedience, but rather in curiosity. Nevertheless, he turned toward
God, and that's what mattered. As he did so, he heard a voice,
calling to him from the fire, *"Moses, Moses,"* and Moses answered,
*"Here I am"* (Exodus 3:4).

> *Then He [God] said, "Do not draw near this place. Take
> your sandals off your feet, for the place where you stand
> is holy ground." Moreover He said, "I am the God of your
> father the God of Abraham, the God of Isaac, and the God
> of Jacob." And Moses hid his face, for he was afraid to
> look upon God.*
> —Exodus 3:5–6

What an experience that must have been! After 40 years of living
in the wilderness, tending his father-in-law's sheep and living
a very simple life, Moses was confronted by the very Creator
of the universe, the God of the Hebrews—the God of Moses's
mother, Jochebed. He was terrified—and well he should be. For
it was here that God gave Moses his marching orders: *"I will
send you to Pharaoh that you may bring My people, the children
of Israel, out of Egypt"* (Exodus 3:10).

It can be a terrifying experience to discover God's purpose
for your life, whatever your age and whatever the circumstances,
for God doesn't necessarily call us to do things that we can do on
our own. He gives us assignments that are too big for us so we
will know that we need Him to fulfill them. And that's what God
wanted Moses to understand. When Moses began to protest his

inability to perform the task God had given him, the Lord said, *"I will certainly be with you. And this shall be a sign to you that I have sent you: When you have brought the people out of Egypt, you shall serve God on this mountain"* (Exodus 3:12).

*"I will certainly be with you."* What a promise! It was the same promise that undoubtedly sustained Jochebed when she allowed her heart to be ripped in two as she placed her beloved son in the care of another woman. It was the promise Moses would prove over and over again as he faced the Egyptian Pharaoh and demanded that the angry ruler release God's people to leave Egypt and to go to their own land to worship the one and only true God. It was the promise that Moses continued to prove even after he had succeeded in leading the Hebrew people out of Egypt and then led them through the wilderness for another 40 years. It was the promise he heard echoing in his ears when he went to the top of the mountain to receive God's Law for the people. And it is the promise we each must cling to as we seek to fulfill the great calling and purpose God has for our lives.

*"I will certainly be with you."* Can you imagine how tightly Moses had to cling to those words as he led his people on dry land through the rolled backwaters of the Red Sea? But do you think that was any more frightening to this man of God than it was for his dear mother when she made that papyrus hideaway for her tiny son and placed him among the reeds of the Nile River? It was the certainty that God was with them that enabled this mother and son to fulfill their destinies, and it is that same certainty that enables us to fulfill ours—and that of our children.

*The power of a mother's prayers isn't limited to geographical distances or life circumstances.*

The power of a mother's love and prayers isn't limited to geographical distance or life circumstances. Jochebed's baby arrived in this world in the midst of an edict that, apart from God's intervention, would have meant the boy's death. Jochebed sacrificed herself to give her son a chance to grow up and become the man God had destined him to be, and surely she must have prayed for him at every point of her often lonely and painful existence. Did she ever get to hold her son close and tell him of her love for him? Did she ever have the joy of hearing him call her "Mother"? More unanswered questions. But even if it was from her eventual vantage point in heaven, she had the joy of knowing that her prayers had been answered, and her son had grown to manhood and fulfilled his destiny. The Hebrew nation was delivered from slavery, and the Law was given on the mountaintop.

Jochebed missed out on a lot that most mothers take for granted, but she was not a failure as a woman or a mother. She loved completely, passionately, selflessly—enough to give up the object of her love to achieve a higher purpose. The God of Abraham, Isaac, and Jacob looked down on her sacrifice...and smiled. Jochebed was a good mother indeed.

*"There is no greater calling in all the world than teaching a child how to live."*
—Dayle Shockley, author

## Something to Think About/
## Enter in Your Journal:

1. What times in your life have you been called on to exhibit selfless love, and what were the results?

2. What people can you think of who modeled that sort of selfless love in your life? Give some examples.

3. In studying Jochebed and Moses's relationship, what parallels do you see to relationships with your children (or with others if you have no children of your own)?

*"No one in the world
can take the place of your mother."*
**—Harry Truman, US President**

## A Mother's Prayer:

*Father, thank You so much for the parental model of selfless love You have given us by offering Your Son to die in our place. Help me to appreciate the depth of that sacrifice on my behalf, the extent of Your pain as You watched Your only Son die for the sins of the world. Please give me a heart of selfless love for others. In Your name. Amen.*

**"As a mother who gave up a baby for adoption, Jochebed is always a comfort to me. Though I did not get to nurse my daughter or watch her from afar, I feel with Jochebed's mother's heart as she watches Moses float away to an uncertain future. All mothers feel this at some point—the release of a child to an uncertain world with faith in an everlasting God. That, I think, is the true test of motherhood."**
**—Marilynn Griffith, author**

*"Her dignity consists in being unknown to the world; her glory is in the esteem of her husband; her pleasures in the happiness of her family."*

—Jean Rousseau, Genevan philosopher, composer, author

# CHAPTER 6

# Hannah: Woman of Prayer, Gratitude, and Integrity

*"For this child I prayed, and the LORD has granted me my petition which I asked of Him. Therefore I also have lent him to the LORD; as long as he lives he shall be lent to the LORD."*
—1 Samuel 1:27–28

SUGGESTED SCRIPTURE READINGS:
1 Samuel 1–2

Second only to Mary, the mother of Jesus, Hannah is often considered the most self-sacrificing mother in the Bible. In fact, some think her prayer of dedication to the Lord may have influenced Mary's own attitude and life. Regardless of whether or not that's true, we can't deny Hannah's life of prayer and integrity.

Hannah was a humble woman with a heart for God and a deep love and respect for her husband. She also had a relatively comfortable lifestyle, as evidenced by the type of sacrifices she and her family offered at the tabernacle. But even with all that, she was not a content or fulfilled woman. Something was missing, and that something was a child—in particular, a son. In a culture where sons were the mark of an honored and esteemed mother, this was an especially difficult and trying situation.

To further complicate matters, Hannah's husband had a second wife named Peninnah, who had provided several children to the household, and this second wife was no gracious friend or sister to Hannah. In fact, she mocked and ridiculed Hannah's childlessness. So in addition to the pain of having no children, Hannah had to endure her rival's verbal assaults. And yet, despite her trials, Hannah chose to become a woman of prayer and integrity, a worthy role model for those of us who would follow in her footsteps.

❖ ❖ ❖

Is it truly possible to follow in the footsteps of one who lived so many generations earlier, in such a foreign and unfamiliar culture? Absolutely! As we examine Hannah's life more closely, we will find some amazing similarities to our own.

I haven't personally struggled with childlessness, though I have a cousin who did, and eventually she and her husband adopted three beautiful children. I've struggled with other issues of barrenness, though, and I imagine you have too—issues that were ongoing and painful, issues that provoked ridicule and mockery from others, issues that made us wonder if God would ever hear and respond. And that's where Hannah's role-modeling comes in.

*Hannah prayed continually.*

Hannah didn't just pray a few times or even for a year or two; she prayed continually, year after year, offering sacrifices and making vows to God. And she did this in the face of almost overwhelming odds and nearly impossible obstacles. Through it all, she remained a woman of prayer. And when those prayers were finally answered, she showed herself a woman of integrity by keeping her vow to God, even though it entailed great personal sacrifice on her part.

## Seeking God

When we first meet Hannah in the opening chapter of 1 Samuel (a book which bears the name of her firstborn son), we find she is married to an Ephraimite named Elkanah, who had a second wife named Peninnah, who, according to verse 2, had children, while Hannah did not.

Quite obviously Hannah lived in polygamous times, times where the morals of Israel had become lax. And yet her husband continued to bring his family to Shiloh to offer their yearly sacrifices at the tabernacle (or tent-form of the future) temple.

Hannah also lived in perilous political times, when the Israelite tribes were oppressed by their more powerful neighbors, the Philistines. Yet political or cultural concerns were certainly not at the top of Hannah's priority list. This young woman was much more caught up in the pain and social repercussions of being childless. Despite the fact that she was married to a man who obviously loved her and even favored her over his other wife, Hannah could think of little else than the burning desire within her to have a child.

Hannah, of course, isn't the first woman we read of in the Bible who was childless. Sarah, Rebekah, and Rachel all went through periods of barrenness and, in their own way, beseeched God for a child. Sarah, however, laughed when she heard the announcement that she was finally going to have a baby, while Rebekah depended on her husband, Isaac, to seek God for her. Rachel reacted much the same way, declaring to her husband, Jacob, *"Give me children or I'll die!"* Hannah, on the other hand, went to God herself, humbly yet ardently imploring the One who opens and shuts wombs to grant her the honor of motherhood.

In verse 3 of this opening chapter of 1 Samuel, we see Elkanah, along with his two wives and the rest of his household, arriving in

Shiloh for the annual sacrifice. That verse tells us that the priests, Eli, and his two sons, Hophni and Phinehas, were there. In the next two verses we read that:

> *Whenever the time came for Elkanah to make an offering, he would give portions to Peninnah his wife and to all her sons and daughters. But to Hannah he would give a double portion, for he loved Hannah, although the* LORD *had closed her womb.*
> —1 Samuel 1:4–5

This is evidence of Elkanah's love for Hannah and his favoritism to her over Peninnah, despite the fact that Peninnah had given him children and Hannah had not. As a result of this obvious favoritism, however, Peninnah held great resentment and contempt toward the woman she considered her rival, and she repaid Hannah with taunts and jeers about her inability to produce and bear a child. Verses 6 and 7 tell us that Peninnah's hostility toward Hannah was so intense that it made Hannah miserable to the point that she was in tears and no longer wanted to eat.

Poor Elkanah, an obviously caring and considerate husband, said to Hannah in verse 8, *"Hannah, why do you weep? Why do you not eat? And why is your heart grieved? Am I not better to you than ten sons?"*

Those must have been some tough questions for Hannah to answer. How could she tell her husband that though she appreciated his love and concern, the truth was that he was not better to her than ten sons? And so, we are told in verses 9 and 10, she arose and went to the tabernacle, where she *"prayed to the* LORD *and wept in anguish"* (1 Samuel 1:10). And then, in verse 11, we read of her great vow to the Lord:

> *"O* LORD *of hosts, if You will indeed look on the affliction of Your maidservant and remember me, and not forget Your maidservant, but will give Your maidservant a male child, then I will give him to the* LORD *all the days of his life, and no razor shall come upon his head."*

Hannah, who was accustomed to prayer, continued to seek God, even after making this memorable vow. As she did so, the priest Eli watched her. Verse 13 says that *"Hannah spoke in her heart; only her lips moved, but her voice was not heard. Therefore Eli thought she was drunk."*

*How tragic that this poor woman should be suspected of being drunk!*

How tragic that this poor woman, who was humbly and with perseverance seeking God, should be suspected of being drunk! Possibly that tells us something of the low moral standards of the day that a priest would even consider that such a thing was possible, but obviously he did, as in verse 14 he confronted her and said, *"How long will you be drunk? Put your wine away from you!"*

Such an accusation from a priest would be difficult for anyone to process, let alone someone in Hannah's emotional state. And yet, exhibiting her genuine humility, she did not take offense. Instead, she offered this simple but respectful explanation:

*"No, my lord, I am a woman of sorrowful spirit. I have drunk neither wine nor intoxicating drink, but have poured out my soul before the LORD. Do not consider your maidservant a wicked woman, for out of the abundance of my complaint and grief I have spoken until now."*
—1 Samuel 1:15–16

Apparently it was just the right answer, for verse 17 quotes Eli as responding, *"Go in peace, and the God of Israel grant your petition which you have asked of Him."*

Finally, in verse 18, Hannah says to Eli, *"Let your maidservant find favor in your sight."* And then, her business with God concluded, she goes home and has something to eat, and *"her face was no longer sad"* (1 Samuel 1:18).

Not only was Hannah a woman who knew how to pray, but she was also a woman who knew how to trust God for the answer. She had laid her heartache and desire at God's feet, knowing He alone could bring the right answer, and then she went on about her business.

In verse 19 we move immediately to the next phase of Hannah's life: She and Elkanah are back home, and *"Elkanah knew Hannah his wife,"* meaning they had sexual relations. Then, also in this verse, we read, *"and the LORD remembered her [Hannah]."*

This doesn't mean, of course, that God had forgotten Hannah, though there are times we all feel a bit that way. We've been praying for a breakthrough—whether it's finally having a baby, seeing a prodigal return home, an ill child become well, a husband commit his life to the Lord, or financial needs met—and we wonder if God has truly forgotten our name. *How long, Lord? How long do I pray? How long do I wait? Everyone else has these blessings, Lord. Why not me?*

But we are never told that Hannah reacted in that way. Instead, year after year, she humbly entreated God to open her womb and to grant her a child. She fully recognized that God was the giver of all life and her only hope for a baby. She didn't whine or complain or rail against the injustices of having to share her husband with Peninnah and the fact that Peninnah had children while she didn't; she just kept praying—asking, seeking, knocking—until she had peace that God would answer in His way and in His time.

And so He did. He "remembered" Hannah and opened her womb. Verse 20 says that *"it came to pass in the process of time that Hannah conceived and bore a son, and called his name Samuel, saying, 'Because I have asked for him from the LORD.'"* Hannah was so grateful that God had answered her prayers and given her a son that she wanted that son's name to reflect her gratitude. And so she called him Samuel, a reminder to everyone who heard his name that he was a blessing from God and that she publicly acknowledged having received him from the Lord's hand.

This was no small gesture on Hannah's part. How easy it would have been to give him one of numerous family names, or even to name him after his earthly father, Elkanah, but Hannah resisted the temptation that we all face at times: to take credit ourselves for something God has done.

It's an easy trap to fall into, isn't it? We pray and pray, wondering at times if God is even listening, and then, finally, He answers—and soon we forget how desperately we depended on God while we awaited that answer. Before long we begin to act as if we'd accomplished something on our own, and our "attitude of gratitude" begins to fade. Could Hannah have done that? Of course! How about the umpteenth night in a row without any sleep? Do you suppose she might have finally drifted off, only to be awakened less than an hour later by a crying baby, and been tempted to complain about her lack of sleep, to grumble about listening to her husband snore contentedly while she walked the floor and tried to keep her eyes open?

*It's easy to slip into that complaining mode and forget.*

Those of us with children have been there, haven't we? And when our sleep is interrupted, time and again, night after night, it's easy to slip into that complaining mode and forget what a great blessing and responsibility God has given us. And possibly even Hannah had a few moments like that—but I doubt they lasted long. One look at her precious Samuel and she remembered the days, weeks, months, and even years of seeking God for a child, of listening to Peninnah's taunts, of watching other women nurse and pamper their children while she had none. How many times, as she rocked and nursed her precious baby, did she remember that prayer of dedication, that vow to the Lord in the temple (tabernacle) at Shiloh? How many times did she marvel at God's faithfulness and generosity to answer?

Oh yes, this woman of prayer was also a woman of gratitude, who never forgot who it was that had blessed her to be a mother. But mixed with that gratitude was a memory of her vow to give her child back to the Lord—for the rest of his life. It was not a vow she made lightly, and not one she could dismiss or ignore...no matter how much she might want to do so.

But did she want to? Did Hannah regret having made such a vow to the Lord? If so, the Bible doesn't mention it. We are never told that Hannah looked for a way to renege on her promise. Hannah's vow to God was more than the typical foxhole prayer of "Get me out of here, God, and I'll never do anything bad again!" Hannah was very serious when she prayed and promised her son to God, and Jewish law made no provision or allowance for a woman to negate or nullify her own vows.

For her husband, however, there was such a provision, and we have to assume that at some point Hannah told Elkanah about her vow. At that point, according to Numbers 30:6–8, Elkanah had a decision to make:

> *If indeed she takes a husband, while bound by her vows or by a rash utterance from her lips by which she bound herself, and her husband hears it, and makes no response to her on the day that he hears, then her vows shall stand, and her agreements by which she bound herself shall stand. But if her husband overrules her on the day that he hears it, he shall make void her vow which she took and what she uttered with her lips, by which she bound herself, and the LORD will release her.*

According to the law, on the very day that Elkanah first became aware of Hannah's vow, he could override it. If he chose not to, the vow would stand. Though the Scriptures don't mention Elkanah's decision, we can assume that he chose not to nullify Hannah's vow because the next year, when it was time for the household to go to Shiloh for the annual sacrifice, Hannah begged off, telling her husband that she wanted to stay home with Samuel until he was weaned; then, she said, after he was weaned, *"I will take him, that he may appear before the LORD and remain there forever"* (1 Samuel 1:22). Quite obviously Elkanah was already aware of Hannah's vow and had agreed to it because he replied, *"Do what seems best to you; wait until you have weaned him. Only let the L*ORD *establish His word"* (1 Samuel 1:23).

This exchange speaks of a woman who was not only prayerful and thankful, but also one who dearly loved her son and cherished every moment with him. She knew she would soon give him up to be raised at the tabernacle by the priest, but she wanted to enjoy her time with him while she could. Elkanah, being the ever-considerate husband that he was, readily understood and agreed, even as he reinforced their future commitment to honor Hannah's vow and *"let the L*ORD *establish His word."*

And so it was that dear Hannah stayed home with her little son while the rest of the household went to Shiloh. Later, when Samuel was weaned, *"she took him up with her, with three bulls, one ephah [measure] of flour, and a skin of wine, and brought him to the house of the L*ORD *in Shiloh. And the child was young"* (1 Samuel 1:24).

> *No mother parts with a child—for any reason—without pain.*

We aren't told about any of the emotional struggles this mother went through on this trip, but it's unimaginable that her heart wasn't breaking every step of the way. No mother parts with a child—for any reason—without pain. But that doesn't mean she regretted her vow. In fact, in the next verse we see that they (1 Samuel 2:11 makes it clear that Elkanah was with Hannah and Samuel) *"slaughtered a bull, and brought the child to Eli"* (1 Samuel 1:25). The next three verses tell us more clearly than any others what an honorable and faithful woman Hannah was:

> *And she said, "O my lord! As your soul lives, my lord, I am the woman who stood by you here, praying to the L*ORD. *For this child I prayed, and the L*ORD *has granted me my petition which I asked of Him. Therefore I also have lent him to the L*ORD; *as long as he lives he shall be lent to the L*ORD.*" So they worshiped the L*ORD *there.*
> —1 Samuel 1:26–28

*"For this child I prayed,"* Hannah said to Eli, *"and the LORD has granted me my petition which I asked of Him. Therefore...."* Hannah didn't cry or scream or beg the priest or her husband—or even God—to forget her vow and let her keep her child. Instead she graciously and wholeheartedly gave God all the glory and credit for answering her prayer and providing her with this child, even if it meant she had to give his care over to someone else. And then they—Elkanah, Eli, and Hannah—worshipped God together.

Though the situations are quite different, the selflessness of Hannah is much like that of a woman who, for whatever reason, realizes she is unable to properly care for her child and lovingly gives him up for adoption, to be raised by others who can more readily care for him. It is a gift of love, given from a breaking but selfless heart that cares more for another than for self.

In Hannah's situation, of course, she was giving Samuel over to be raised in service to the Lord—the very Lord who had given Samuel to Hannah and to whom she was extremely grateful. For that reason, and also because she knew it was a great honor to be dedicated to serving God, Hannah was able to release her son with open hands and a joyous, if aching, heart. It was the

> *Her influence on Samuel would not end when she handed him over.*

right thing to do, and Hannah was a woman concerned with doing what was right.

How can we know Hannah rejoiced in fulfilling her vow? The opening verse in chapter 2 confirms it: *"And Hannah prayed and said: 'My heart rejoices in the LORD; my horn is exalted in the LORD. I smile at my enemies, because I rejoice in Your salvation'"* (1 Samuel 2:1). Though her mother's heart was broken, her spirit rejoiced to know her son would spend his life serving the one true God, the God of Israel, who had opened her womb and gifted her with Samuel. Hannah's prayer, uttered as she gave over her son to God's service, is one of the greatest recorded in all the Bible. In fact, many believe it may have been the precursor to the Magnificat prayed by Mary when she learned she would be the mother of the Messiah.

What a godly example Hannah must have been to Samuel throughout her lifetime. Though she held him in her arms for only a very short time, her influence on Samuel would not end when she handed him over to Eli the priest. In fact, verse 19 tells us that *"His [Samuel's] mother used to make him a little robe, and bring it to him year by year when she came up with her husband to offer the yearly sacrifice."* Can you imagine the love that went into the making of those special robes? It's easy to picture Hannah holding the material in her lap, praying and even singing as she worked, each stitch a labor of love.

And then, of course, as they made the annual trip to Shiloh, her heart urged her on, encouraging her as she pictured their meeting and how she would be able to hold her son in her arms once again. It must have been a poignant scene for everyone involved, as mother and son, then father and son, embraced. The Scriptures aren't clear as to how long their visits were, but we can be certain that Hannah cherished each moment and reviewed them countless times after she returned home.

But Hannah's story doesn't end there. Verse 20 tells us that each year Eli would bless Elkanah and his wife, saying, *"The LORD give you descendants from this woman for the loan that was given to the LORD."* Eli was petitioning God on Elkanah and Hannah's behalf to honor their sacrifice of Samuel and give them more children. God, in His graciousness and mercy, answered Eli's petition, as we see in verse 21: *"And the LORD visited Hannah, so that she conceived and bore three sons and two daughters. Meanwhile the child Samuel grew before the LORD."* Even as Samuel *"grew before the LORD"* in the sacred structure under Eli's care, God was blessing Elkanah and Hannah with more children. Elkanah already had children with his other wife, Peninnah, but notice that Eli specifically asked God to grant Elkanah *"descendants from this woman [Hannah] for the loan [Samuel] that was given to the LORD."* Elkanah and Hannah had three more sons after Samuel, and two daughters as well. Theirs was a full household indeed!

Of course, even three sons and two daughters didn't take away the place in Hannah's heart that was reserved for her firstborn, Samuel. Those of us who have more than one child know that one child can never replace another, but we can certainly love each equally. Samuel, however, would always be Hannah's child of promise. *"For this child I prayed,"* Hannah said in 1 Samuel 1:27–28, *"and the LORD has granted me my petition which I asked of Him. Therefore I also have lent him to the LORD; as long as he lives he shall be lent to the LORD."*

Oh, that we would remember Hannah's example when we've prayed long and hard, weeping in intercession, and then seen God answer mercifully and miraculously! That we would have grateful hearts, hearts of integrity that would not turn back from fulfilling our vows to the faithful God who lovingly meets our every need! That we would take time to stop and thank God for every answered prayer, to acknowledge that *"every good gift and every perfect gift is from above, and comes down from the Father of lights, with whom there is no variation or shadow of turning"* (James 1:17). And that we would then say, "Therefore…." God's gifts to us, His answered prayers, require a response of gratitude and integrity on our part, even if, like Hannah, it requires self-sacrifice in the process.

*God's gifts to us, His answered prayers, require a response of gratitude and integrity.*

Hannah's example and legacy to us all is to become women of prayer, women of gratitude, and women of integrity, and to turn over to our faithful God the very things that are most precious to us here on earth—even and especially our beloved children—so that He may fulfill His purpose and bring glory to His name, in and through our lives—and theirs.

> *"In all my efforts to learn to read, my mother shared fully my ambition and sympathized with me and aided me in every way she could. If I have done anything in life worth attention, I feel sure that I inherited the disposition from my mother."*
> —Booker T. Washington, author, educator

## Something to Think About/
## Enter in Your Journal:

1. What are some of the issues you have taken to God in prayer, time and time again, over the years, including prayers concerning your children? Which have you seen answered, and which are you continuing to pray about even today?

2. Consider those times when God has answered your prayers or blessed you in some way and you neglected to thank Him and give Him all the glory and credit for those answered prayers and blessings. Take some time now to review those times and properly thank God for His faithfulness to you and to those in your family.

3. Review the times in your life when you may have showed less than complete and unblemished integrity in handling situations regarding your faith. Have you made vows to God or others and then not fulfilled them? What do you suppose were the reasons you reneged on your promise? Take some time to seek God's forgiveness for those lapses in integrity.

*"Sometimes a mother feels as if her work is in vain. But be patient. If you have planted seeds of love and virtue in the heart of a child, the harvest will be rewarding."*
**—Dayle Shockley, author**

# A MOTHER'S PRAYER

*Father, thank You for the godly example You have
provided to us through the life of Hannah—both as a
woman and as a mother. Thank You for making her a
woman of prayer, gratitude, and integrity. Help me,
Lord, to learn from Hannah's example and to become
more like her in my own life. Turn my heart toward You
daily, Father, so that I might seek You first in all things;
that I might persevere in prayer, even when it seems
that answers will never come; that I might remember to
express my gratitude to You and others when the answers
do come; and that I might exhibit complete integrity
in following through on all my promises and vows that
I have made to You and to others, according to Your
purpose and Your Word. Thank You, Lord.
In Jesus's name. Amen.*

**"Little did I know that the birth experience, filled with
both tremendous joy and excruciating pain,
would be a symbolic forerunner of the mother/child
relationship itself...."**
**—Judy Dippel, author**

"*Grown don't mean nothing to a mother. A child is a child. They get bigger, older, but grown? What's that suppose to mean? In my heart, it don't mean a thing.*"

—from *Beloved* by Toni Morrison, author

# CHAPTER 7

# Rizpah:
# Grief-Stricken
# yet Faithful

*Now Rizpah the daughter of Aiah took sackcloth and spread it for herself on the rock, from the beginning of harvest until the late rains poured on them from heaven. And she did not allow the birds of the air to rest on them by day nor the beasts of the field by night.*
—2 Samuel 21:10

SUGGESTED SCRIPTURE READINGS:
2 Samuel 3:7; 21:1–14

Is there anything more painful—or more seemingly out of the natural order of things—than for a parent to stand at the graveside of a child, grieving over the loss of one more beloved than life itself, one who should have outlived the parent by decades? To give life to a tiny human being, to nurture and bond with that life, and then to see it come to a tragic end, regardless of the circumstances, has to be one of the most difficult challenges any human being can ever face. For those who have experienced it, there are no words adequate to describe the depth of pain and loss; for those who have not, there is no way to truly empathize with the mourner.

Rizpah would understand. She would empathize as few others could, because in a single day she lost not only one child but two—her only two—as well as five other relatives. And none of it was through any fault of her own. Rizpah was simply a victim of circumstance, a political pawn who paid the ultimate price. Yet grief-stricken as she was, she remained faithful to the end.

❖ ❖ ❖

Rizpah lived at a time and in a culture where women had few rights. She was, in fact, a concubine, or "secondary wife," to Saul, the first king of Israel, and though she had even less status or influence than a "primary wife," Rizpah bore two children to Saul—sons named Armoni and Mephibosheth. Though we don't have much personal information about Rizpah or her sons, we know enough to be certain that she loved them dearly.

*Her faithful testimony to a mother's undying love has inspired countless stories through the years.*

Rizpah's name, in fact, is nearly synonymous with the ultimate grieving mother. Though she is mentioned in only a few verses in the Bible, celebrated artists have memorialized her suffering on canvas, and her faithful testimony to a mother's undying love has inspired countless stories through the years. Such a powerful example of motherhood is well worth studying.

## A FAITHFUL CONCUBINE

Our first mention in the Bible about Rizpah is in 2 Samuel 3:7, which simply states, *"And Saul had a concubine, whose name was Rizpah, the daughter of Aiah."* This very basic statement serves only to establish relational ties, in that Rizpah was King Saul's concubine, and she was also the daughter of Aiah. Historical accounts tell us she lived in and around 1025 B.C., and a word study of the name Rizpah reveals the meaning of her seemingly unusual name—unusual at least, to our modern, Western-culture ears—to be something like "glowing coal." Since names meant something in those days, we have to believe there is significance to her title—possibly that hers was a light that continued to burn long after others had burned out, an explanation that becomes more probable as we study this amazing mother.

In that same verse in 2 Samuel, right after we are told that Rizpah was the concubine of King Saul and the daughter of Aiah, we read a somewhat shocking statement: *"So Ishbosheth said to Abner, 'Why have you gone in to my father's concubine?'"* (2 Samuel 3:7). To understand this insulting question, we need to go back to the first part of the first verse in this chapter, which reads, *"Now there was a long war between the house of Saul and the house of David"* (2 Samuel 3:1). Then we move on to verse 6, just prior to our introduction to Rizpah: *"Now it was so, while there was war between the house of Saul and the house of David, that Abner was strengthening his hold on the house of Saul."*

*Her name is linked to the fall and rise of kingdoms.*

Rizpah may have been a concubine with little power of her own, and yet her name is linked to the fall and rise of kingdoms. The houses, or families, of Saul and David had been fighting for years, with Saul doing everything possible to prevent David from taking over his rightful kingship of Israel. Once Saul died, his commanding general, Abner, placed one of Saul's sons, Ishbosheth, on the throne. The tribe of Judah, however, refused to recognize Ishbosheth as king and instead anointed David as their regent, effectively splitting Israel into two kingdoms.

It seemed that Abner would be successful in his attempts to preserve the majority of the kingdom for Saul's heirs—until Ishbosheth heard a rumor that Abner had "gone in to"—or had sexual relations with—Saul's concubine, Rizpah. If the rumor were true, this was a serious affront and an even more serious threat to Ishbosheth, as it could imply that Abner intended to try to usurp Ishbosheth's new position as king and take the throne for himself.

Because of Abner's highly indignant response, however, we can assume that the rumor probably wasn't true:

> *"Am I a dog's head that belongs to Judah? Today I show loyalty to the house of Saul your father, to his brothers, and to his friends, and have not delivered you into the hand of David; and you charge me today with a fault concerning this woman? May God do so to Abner, and more also, if I do not do for David as the LORD has sworn to him—to transfer the kingdom from the house of Saul, and set up the throne of David over Israel and over Judah, from Dan to Beersheba."*
> —2 Samuel 3:8–10

In addition to Abner's denial of having had relations with Rizpah, it was quite obvious that Abner was angered because he had worked so hard to honor Saul's memory and establish Ishbosheth as king. As a result, Abner turned on Ishbosheth and all of Saul's house, and he immediately began negotiating with David to transfer the entire kingdom of Israel to him.

Regardless of the basis or motivation for this apparently false rumor regarding Rizpah, the mere mention of it was enough to change the entire history of Israel, therefore ascribing a lot more influence to this otherwise powerless concubine than even she may have realized. Rizpah knew only that the father of her two sons, the former king of Israel and the man she had considered her husband, was now dead. According to the custom of the time, she now belonged to Saul's son Ishbosheth, whether he wanted her or not. Her fate lay in his hands, and it was a fragile place, at best, to rest her hope and security.

Rizpah did, however, have two sons by King Saul, Armoni and Mephibosheth, and in those days, when a woman was widowed, it was up to her sons to care for her, regardless of her position in society. With a famine in the land, their care for her was even more crucial to her survival.

Skipping ahead to the 21st chapter of 2 Samuel, we read that King David was extremely concerned about this famine, which had lasted for three years. When David inquired of the Lord why they continued to suffer from this famine, the Lord answered, *"It is because of Saul and his bloodthirsty house, because he killed the Gibeonites"* (2 Samuel 21:1).

Approximately 400 years earlier, not long after the death of Moses, when Joshua served as leader of the Israelites, the Gibeonites had tricked Joshua and the other leaders into making a treaty with them. Though they had procured the treaty through deceit, the leaders of Israel had honored that treaty for centuries, allowing the Gibeonites to live in the land, even though they did so as virtual servants to the Israelites. At some point in Saul's reign, he decided to break the treaty and tried—though unsuccessfully—to completely wipe out the Gibeonites. God was not pleased. Despite the fact that the treaty had been secured through false means, God quite obviously expected the Israelites to honor it.

*When a woman was widowed, it was up to her sons to care for her.*

When King David realized that God was punishing all of Israel for Saul's sins, he went to the Gibeonites to try to make things right. They told him they weren't interested in financial compensation; the only way David and Israel could atone for Saul's sin was through the shedding of blood—specifically through the death of seven of Saul's descendants. David agreed, and he turned over to the Gibeonites five of Saul's grandsons, as well as Armoni and Mephibosheth, the two sons of Saul's concubine, Rizpah, all of whom had personally been involved in Saul's war against the Gibeonites. The Gibeonites would be allowed to extract revenge against Saul by executing his descendants.

And so, during the harvest season, Armoni and Mephibosheth, Rizpah's only children and the sole source of her support, were hanged by the Gibeonites—along with Saul's five grandsons—and there was absolutely nothing this poor mother could do to stop it.

## A FAITHFUL GUARDIAN AND PROTECTOR

As a result of the executions of Saul's seven relatives, God's judgment on Israel was fulfilled, and the famine eventually stopped as we will see. In addition to being one of the key players (albeit unwillingly) to the fall of one kingdom and the rise of another in Israel—Saul's and David's—Rizpah was also a key player in the drama of Israel's reconciliation with the Gibeonites and, more importantly, with God. But this woman who had once dressed in silk and lived in a palace as the king's concubine was now left with nothing but a broken heart and a bereaved spirit. The only injury that could be added to this bereft woman's tragedy would soon follow, when her sons' bodies

*It was the last act of love she could show to her grown children.*

were left to rot in the sun and be eaten by the birds of the air and the beasts of the field. And that was just more than this devastated mother could endure.

And so she positioned herself at the site of her sons' demise, the rock where the seven gallows stood as a stark reminder of the price of broken vows, and she stood guard over their corpses— day and night, for five months—as the stench of death increased until she could smell little else. Now that's dedication! Through the heat of the day and cool of the night, Rizpah didn't budge. It was the last act of love she could show to her grown children, and she was determined to do it well.

Her first deed was to spread sackcloth, which was symbolic of grief and death and loss, over the area where the gallows had been erected. Some have suggested that she even made a tent of sackcloth to place over the bodies of her dead sons, which is quite possible, as the sackcloth of Old Testament times was made of a coarse cloth woven from the hair of goats and camels. In her book, *All of the Women of the Bible*, Edith Deen suggests that when Rizpah spread the sackcloth over her sons' bodies, she may have made a pledge to God that she would watch over them until the rains came, indicating the end of God's judgment and the famine in the land.

In any event, it was a long and relentless vigil—five months of grieving her loss and fighting to protect what was left. She had nothing except her sons' bodies, and she wasn't about to let them be devoured or dragged off by predators, as evidenced in 2 Samuel 21:10: *"She did not allow the birds of the air to rest on them by day nor the beasts of the field by night."* Rizpah was determined to stay put until the situation changed and she could give her sons a proper burial, one befitting the offspring of a former king and his family. And so, alone and bereaved, Rizpah sat, day after lonely day, night after frightening night, guarding the rotting, decaying bodies of her loved ones.

What a picture she must have presented to those who passed by! Curious onlookers no doubt stopped to gawk, at least at first, but after a few weeks, word had spread about the "crazy woman" who refused to leave her dead children. And though some may have stopped to pity or ridicule her, others quite possibly came to cheer her on and encourage her. Some must have gone so far as to provide for her needs, bringing her food and water, since she would have had no other source of sustenance during those long months of vigil and mourning.

Though Rizpah's actions seem extreme, particularly to our Western mindset, they may not be as unimaginable as they appear at first glance. Have you ever known a mother—or a father, for that matter—who lost a child? The grief of loss would be bad enough, but what of a mother who has no body to bury, no gravesite to visit, no headstone to decorate? There is no easy way to lose a child, nothing to ease the excruciating pain, but a proper funeral or memorial service and burial brings a certain feeling of closure, a needed sense of dignity and honor to the child who is gone from the mother's arms—but never from her heart.

Jan Coates knows about that sort of loss—and the stunning sense of grief that overwhelms the human spirit. On the night the Missouri Highway Patrol trooper knocked on her door and asked, "Is this your son's wallet, ma'am?" she thought her life was over. As the news that her teenaged son, Chris— her only child—had been killed by a drunk driver sank in, she collapsed on the floor and curled into a fetal position. With her head tucked in and her knees tightly packed against her chest, she whispered, "Please, God, I need You. If You're there, God...can we talk?" Then blackness closed in, and for a few moments she slipped into sweet oblivion.

*She collapsed on the floor and curled into a fetal position.*

True, Jan didn't have to stand vigil over her son's body for five months, protecting it from wild beasts while awaiting a proper burial, but she experienced that same sense of loss and grief that Rizpah must have felt, as well as the feeling that things were out of order. Children aren't supposed to die first; parents aren't supposed to have to bury their children. We all expect to have to bury our parents one day, but our children? Never!

How do parents survive such tragedies? How did Jan handle it?

As she lay on the floor and darkness closed in, she slipped into another world, a world where she existed in a heavenly dream, standing with her son, Chris, in heaven. "How indescribably wonderful that was!" she remembers now, knowing it was God's mercy giving her a glimpse of the joy Chris was already experiencing in the presence of his Lord and the joy Jan and Chris would someday experience when they both rejoice around the heavenly throne.

But on earth, she would still have to bear the pain, still have to try to make sense of the senseless, to remain hopeful when all hope was seemingly gone. Family, friends, and loved ones rallied around her, walking with her when she couldn't walk alone— carrying her when she couldn't walk at all. But it was her pastor, who came to visit and pray with her several days after Chris's funeral, who truly helped Jan begin her healing process.

"Father, You know the pain of losing a child," the pastor prayed. "Your Son was killed—not by a drunk driver but by men filled with hate and rage. God, only You can comfort Jan as she mourns the loss of her only child."

Though Rizpah lived in Old Testament days, there is more correlation with the death of Jesus than might seem apparent. Jesus hung between the earth and the heavens, a sacrifice not for His own sins—He was sinless—but for the sins of others, as the price for peace and reconciliation with God was paid once and for all. In Rizpah's case, not only was she concerned about watching over and protecting her sons' bodies until they could receive a proper burial, but she also understood that they had been strung up to die, not for their own sins but to atone for the sins of others—all the more reason that she would not forsake them until their sacrifice had been recognized.

*News of Rizpah's long, dreary vigil reached the ears of the new king.*

And recognized it was, by none other than King David himself. When news of Rizpah's long, dreary vigil reached the ears of the new king, he was moved by her display of grief and faithfulness. He was so moved, in fact, that he went to Jabesh Gilead to collect the bodies, or bones, of Saul and his son Jonathan, who had been David's best friend, closer to him even than his own brothers. The bones of Saul and Jonathan had been taken to Jabesh Gilead after being recovered from the Philistines but had never been placed in the burial spot befitting men of their standing.

David, inspired by Rizpah's dedication, determined to remedy the oversight regarding Saul and Jonathan. After retrieving their bones, he also went on to retrieve the bones of Rizpah's two sons and Saul's five grandsons as well, and then he buried them all in the tomb of Saul's father, Kish, finally assuring a proper and honorable internment for Saul and his offspring. This act by David may also have provided some sort of final reconciliation with the family of the man who had persecuted him for so many years, trying in vain to prevent David from taking his rightful place as king of Israel.

This reconciling of differences between Israel and the Gibeonites, as well as the families of Saul and David, also succeeded in bringing an end to the famine that had plagued the land. Though Rizpah herself is mentioned in no more than a handful of verses, and though she herself had little if any influence or power in the courts of royalty, this one lone woman and her faithful commitment to honor and protect her only children to the very end has won her a place in history books, in paintings, and in the hearts of mothers everywhere who have lost a beloved child.

But what about other mothers, those who have not lost a child to death? Does Rizpah as guardian and protector speak to them as well?

In many ways, Rizpah represents every parent—mother or father—who has lost a child, but there is more. She also represents every parent who has longed for that child's memory to be honored. Rizpah displayed great courage and faithfulness in her lonely vigil, knowing there was nothing she could do to bring her children back but believing she could at least ensure them a proper and honorable burial.

Though nothing can take away the pain of losing a child, there are positive ways to deal with that loss. Jan, for instance, whose only son was killed by a drunk driver, could have spent her life raging at the unfairness of a young, innocent life snuffed out while the perpetrator walked away from the accident unscathed, but she didn't. Though she grieved and mourned for her son, she also became actively involved in MADD (Mothers Against Drunk Drivers), working as an advocate to help others going through similar situations. She has also started a ministry called "Set Free Today" (www.setfreetoday.com) to help others work through pain and loss in their own lives, a biblical principle seen clearly in Job 42:10: *"And the LORD restored Job's losses **when he prayed for his friends**. Indeed the LORD gave Job twice as much as he had before"* (emphasis added).

*Jan, like Job, turned her loss into an opportunity.*

Rather than lose herself in her grief and allow it to turn into bitterness, Jan, like Job, turned her loss into an opportunity to pray for and minister to others, as many parents have done in similar situations. Rizpah's loss was enormous, but so was the eventual outcome—the reconciliation of Israel and the Gibeonites, the end of a famine, and above all else, the reconciliation of Israel to God.

Rizpah's experience, as well as Jan's, also paints a picture of the truth of Romans 8:28: *"And we know that all things work together for good to those who love God, to those who are the called according to His purpose."*

We live in a broken world, in which pain and loss are ever-present realities. But despite the trials and tragedies we might face, God is faithful and can turn those very tragedies into something good—if we will just let Him. But we, like Rizpah—and Jan—must resolve to be faithful and to trust God to bring about that good, regardless of the evil we see around us.

Of course, we can't deny the foreshadowing we see in this picture of innocent blood being shed to bring about reconciliation. That principle has been in effect since the Garden of Eden, when Adam and Eve tried to cover their sin through their own effort, only to discover that God's atonement required the shedding of blood—innocent blood. Since none but Jesus has ever been born sinless or lived a sinless, innocent life, He alone could provide the required atonement for our sins and open the door for humankind to be restored to relationship with the Father.

## Rizpah Remembered

Is it any wonder that even today Rizpah is remembered as a loyal mother, a faithful guardian of her offspring, a protector and defender of their memory? How similar she must have felt to a mother who stands at the graveside of a child who has died defending his or her country, dying honorably to protect loved ones and now, in death, being honored by those served? As the honor guard folds and presents the flag to that grieving mother, her pain doesn't go away, but her heart swells with pride to know her child has not died in vain. And, of course, if that child was a believer who knew and loved Jesus as Savior, she can rejoice that she will see her child once again (see

1 Thessalonians 4:13). For we who know the One who Himself hung between heaven and earth to bring peace between God and man have this great promise to comfort and encourage us:

> *But I do not want you to be ignorant, brethren, concerning those who have fallen asleep, lest you sorrow as others who have no hope. For if we believe that Jesus died and rose again, even so God will bring with Him those who sleep in Jesus. For this we say to you by the word of the Lord, that we who are alive and remain until the coming of the Lord will by no means precede those who are asleep. For the Lord Himself will descend from heaven with a shout, with the voice of an archangel, and with the trumpet of God. And the dead in Christ will rise first. Then we who are alive and remain shall be caught up together with them in the clouds to meet the Lord in the air. And thus we shall always be with the Lord. Therefore comfort one another with these words.*
> —1 Thessalonians 4:13–18

Rizpah could only cling to the promise of Israel's God and look forward to the One who would come to pay the price to bring peace and reconciliation to a world lost in the darkness of sin. Perhaps that is why her name was Rizpah—"glowing coal"— because she was a forerunner of all who would look forward to the hope of the Light of the world who would one day come to dispel that darkness.

> **"A man loves his sweetheart the most,**
> **his wife the best, but his mother the longest."**
> **—Irish Proverb**

## SOMETHING TO THINK ABOUT/
## ENTER IN YOUR JOURNAL:

1. Have you, or someone you know, ever lost a child? Have you ever written in a journal or discussed with someone else what happened and how you—or the person who suffered this great loss—handled the situation? If not, can you attempt to do so now that you've read Rizpah's story?

2. Whether through the loss of a child to death or some other painful experience involving a child, how have you seen the great truth of Romans 8:28—that God brings good out of evil, joy out of sorrow, hope out of loss—played out in your life and/or the lives of those close to you?

3. How can Rizpah's example of dedication and loyalty help you in dealing with some of the most difficult issues in your own life?

*"Making a decision to have a child—it's momentous.*
*It is to decide forever to have your heart go walking*
*around outside your body."*
**—Elizabeth Stone, author**

# A MOTHER'S PRAYER

*Father, thank You for the amazing example of Saul's concubine, Rizpah. Thank You for her loyalty and determination, her faithfulness and courage, her devotion and love for her children. Help me, Lord, to become like Rizpah in my determination to follow You, to serve You, and to be a godly example to others. Teach me, Father, to take the pain and disappointments of my life and allow You to turn them around for good, to minister to others, and to bring You honor and glory. I ask it in Jesus's wonderful name. Amen.*

**"A man's work is from sun to sun,
but a mother's work is never done."
—Author unknown**

*"God didn't give me the kids that I wanted; He gave me the kids that I needed to become the kind of mom whose only option was to trust them to Him."*

—Kathi Lipp, author

# CHAPTER 8

# Bathsheba: Redemption and Restoration

*Then David comforted Bathsheba his wife, and went in to her and lay with her. So she bore a son, and he called his name Solomon. And the LORD loved him.*
—2 Samuel 12:24

SUGGESTED SCRIPTURE READINGS:
2 Samuel 11:1–27; 12:1–24, 31; 1 Kings 1; 2:13–25;
1 Chronicles 3:5; Matthew 1:6

On the surface, it would seem that most mothers today have little in common with Bathsheba, who went from being the wife of a mighty warrior to an adulteress, then the beloved wife of a king and, finally, the honored and respected mother of another king. That may be a bit more notoriety and excitement than most of us would care to have in our lives. However, it's unlikely that Bathsheba purposely planned any of her roles other than the wife of a Hittite soldier named Uriah, a trusted and loyal member of King David's army.

The saga of how this extremely attractive and seemingly intelligent young woman moved from warrior's wife to royalty is one of the most tragic yet redemptive stories in all of history. And, though this unlikely love story was born out of a king's unbridled lust, amazingly, it was nurtured in the grace and forgiveness that can come only from the heart of a merciful God—and eventually came to fruition in the life of one known as the "wisest man who ever lived," King Solomon of Israel.

❖ ❖ ❖

In 2 Samuel 11:1–2, before we ever meet Bathsheba, we are introduced to the circumstances that set this story in motion:

> *It happened  in the spring of the year, **at the time when kings go out to battle,** that David sent Joab and his servants with him, and all Israel; and they destroyed the people of Ammon and besieged Rabbah. **But David remained at Jerusalem.** Then it happened one evening that David arose from his bed and walked on the roof of the king's house. And from the roof **he saw a woman bathing,** and **the woman was very beautiful** to behold* (emphasis added).

The stage is set—for tragedy, but also for redemption. King David, though experienced and skilled in battle and who therefore should have been leading his army into battle, had instead listened to the advice of others—a commander's suggestion—and had chosen to stay behind in the comforts of his palace. As a result, he found himself in the proverbial wrong place at the wrong time—on the rooftop of his palace late one night. When he looked down onto the rooftop, or courtyard, of the house of Uriah, one of David's most loyal warriors, he saw something that would change his life—as well as the lives of many others—for centuries to come. For there, as was the custom of the times, was Uriah's lovely wife, Bathsheba, bathing at a time when she should safely have been able to assume that no one else would be awake or able to see her. Her assumption was wrong, and as a result, her life too was about to change beyond anything she could ever have imagined.

## URIAH'S WIFE; KING DAVID'S LOVER

Little if anything is known about Bathsheba's early life, though it appears that she came from a God-fearing family, since her father's name was Eliam (see 2 Samuel 11:3), (which contains *El*, the shorter form of the name *God*). We also know that she was exceptionally beautiful, as the Hebrew word used to describe Bathsheba indicates. It was that exceptional beauty that drew King David's eye and caused an otherwise godly man to act on his lust, bringing about sins that had far-reaching impact as recorded in the Scriptures.

*David was able to look down from his rooftop into their courtyard.*

The home where Uriah and Bathsheba lived was close enough to the king's palace that David was able to look down from his rooftop into their courtyard. This proximity suggests the possibility that when the nation of Israel was not at war, Uriah may have served as a member of the king's palace guard. In any event, Uriah was a trusted military leader and a valiant warrior.

Some commentators have concluded that Bathsheba was a bit of a wanton or loose woman, an "unfaithful wife waiting to happen," simply because she was bathing in sight of the king's palace and that she then had an adulterous affair with the king. However, there is no Scripture to prove that theory. Many other commentators believe that Bathsheba was nothing more than the beautiful victim of a reigning monarch's lust and power, and there are several verses to uphold that interpretation.

For one thing, as mentioned earlier, it was a common practice or custom for people to bathe on their rooftops/courtyard (often one and the same thing) at night when the chances of anyone seeing them were remote. We can only assume that the moonlight was exceptionally bright that night and that King David's eyesight was exceptionally sharp. Regardless, Bathsheba's outdoor bathing at night was not an unusual act, nor is it sufficient proof of wanton or loose morals on her part. In the cultural setting of the day, she had every right to suppose that her privacy would be respected and there would be no repercussions for her behavior.

The king—who should have been out fighting with his troops—now had other ideas. Second Samuel 11:2 tells us that instead of being where kings were supposed to be, he was walking on the rooftop of his palace, and from there *"he saw a woman bathing, and the woman was very beautiful to behold."* At that point, had David's heart been right with the Lord, he would have turned away and respected the privacy of his trusted soldier's wife—but he didn't. He stayed where he was, and he watched— a dangerous decision when temptation comes our way.

Then, to compound his sin, he acted on the lust in his heart, using his power and position to get what he wanted. He checked around to find out who this beautiful woman might be; when he was told she was Uriah's wife, that should have ended the matter. It didn't. Verse 4 tells us that even when he knew that Bathsheba was married to one of David's military leaders, the selfish king still *"sent messengers, and took her."*

The wording in that verse is very important, as it paints a picture of Bathsheba's abduction from her home and the king's subsequent forcing of himself upon her. In other words, the sexual act that took place as a result of David's having Bathsheba brought from her home to the palace was more than likely a rape—a possibly legally sanctioned one, perhaps, because of his position as king, but a rape nonetheless. Bathsheba wasn't "invited" to the palace; she was "taken" there by the king's messengers. The king was sovereign and could do as he wished, have what he wanted. He wanted Bathsheba, wife of Uriah, and so he took her.

Verse 4 goes on to tell us that the king *"lay with her... and she returned to her house."* Nothing is said of Bathsheba's reaction to being kidnapped from her home, taken to the palace, and forced to have sexual intercourse with the king. The culture she lived in left her little recourse, and possibly that's why her response to this situation isn't recorded. The following verse, however, tells us what happened next: *"And the woman conceived; so she sent and told David, and said, 'I am with child'"* (2 Samuel 11:5).

Now both David and Bathsheba had a problem. Though the king could get away with more than most anyone else, simply because of his position, there were still boundaries of behavior that, when crossed, could bring shame as well as dire consequences. Bathsheba, whose husband was gone and therefore her pregnancy had to have come about as a result of adulterous behavior, could have been stoned to death. David, on the other hand, could suffer irreparable damage to his reputation, as well as his relationship with his military troops and other kingdom subjects. It was a dilemma he needed to resolve quickly.

*The mighty King David then stooped so low.*

Of course, the obvious thing would be to confess his sin and ask forgiveness of all concerned, particularly God. That's always the right choice to make in such a situation. However, we often do otherwise. Like David, we would rather look for a way to "fix" the problem without exposing ourselves. And so the king sent for Uriah, hoping to bring him home from battle so he would go home and have sexual relations with Bathsheba; the pregnancy could then be attributed to Uriah, and the problem would be solved.

Except Uriah didn't exactly follow the king's directions. In 2 Samuel 11:7–9, we see he came home from battle. but because Uriah was an honorable man, David's plan began to quickly unravel.

*When Uriah had come to him, David asked how Joab was doing, and how the people were doing, and how the war prospered. And David said to Uriah, "Go down to your house and wash your feet." So Uriah departed from the*

*king's house, and a gift of food from the king followed him.
But Uriah slept at the door of the king's house with all the
servants of his lord, and did not go down to his house.*

For whatever reason, Uriah chose not to go home that night, and
therefore he had no opportunity to sleep with his wife and fulfill
David's plan. It may have been that Uriah was showing respect for
the law that consecrated warriors for battle and therefore prohibited
them from engaging in sexual intercourse, even with their wives,
author Edith Deen surmises. And so the king tried a second time
to entice Uriah to go home to Bathsheba by getting him drunk
(1 Samuel 11:13). When that attempt also failed, David
compounded his sin and plotted to have Uriah murdered so he
could take Bathsheba for himself—permanently.

The mighty King David then stooped so low as to write a letter
to Joab, his commander in the field, and sent it to Joab by Uriah's
own hand. In it was, in effect, Uriah's death sentence, for the note
instructed Joab, *"Set Uriah in the forefront of the hottest battle, and
retreat from him, that he may be struck down and die"* (2 Samuel
11:15). The honorable Uriah delivered the letter without reading
it; Joab then obeyed his king's orders, and *"Uriah the Hittite died"*
(2 Samuel 11:17).

Again, we are told little of Bathsheba's behavior or reaction to
her husband's death, or even if she ever discovered that he fell at
the orders of the king, but we do know she observed a traditional
mourning time, for verse 26 tells us: *"When the wife of Uriah
heard that Uriah her husband was dead, she mourned for her
husband."* Verse 27 then tells of us King David's actions following
that mourning period: *"And when her mourning was over, David
sent and brought her to his house, and she became his wife and
bore him a son."*

Uriah the Hittite was dead; Bathsheba was now free to marry
the king and legally bear his child. Quite obviously the king was
anxious to have this happen, as he immediately had her brought
to the palace, where they were married. Soon after, their son was
born. But the chapter ends on an ominous note: *"But the thing
that David had done displeased the LORD"* (2 Samuel 11:27).

Mothers of the Bible Speak to Mothers of Today

# KING DAVID'S WIFE

It is important to note here that as David and Bathsheba began their relationship as man and wife, it was David's sin that is recorded as having displeased the Lord—all the more reason to suppose that the physical relationship that initiated this situation was forced upon Bathsheba.

Regardless of its beginnings, however, the relationship had to be a rocky one. It is doubtful that anyone besides Joab knew that the king had purposely ordered Uriah to the front lines, but many—including Bathsheba—may have speculated that such was the case. If so, and if she had cared at all about Uriah, this suspicion was bound to have adversely affected her feelings toward David. Compound that with what was probably a rape that resulted in her pregnancy and, ultimately, Uriah's death, and Bathsheba was sure to have some ill will toward her new husband, no matter how regal or royal he may have been.

So how is it that a marriage that began on such poor footing ended up being such a close and respected relationship?

No doubt the change began with a visit from a man named Nathan.

Immediately following the last comment in chapter 11, *"But the thing that David had done displeased the LORD,"* we read this wonderful opening to chapter 12: *"Then the LORD sent Nathan to David"* (2 Samuel 12:1). Nathan was a prophet who eventually wrote histories of the reigns of both David and Solomon, and who was also involved in the music of the temple.

Isn't that just like God? We do something to displease Him, so what does He do? He immediately moves to reconcile the relationship.

In David's case, God sent a prophet to tell David a story. Here is the story that Nathan delivered:

*"There were two men in one city, one rich and the other poor. The rich man had exceedingly many flocks and herds. But the poor man had nothing, except one little ewe lamb which he had bought and nourished; and it grew up*

*together with him and with his children. It ate of his own food and drank from his own cup and lay in his bosom; and it was like a daughter to him. And a traveler came to the rich man, who refused to take from his own flock and from his own herd to prepare one for the wayfaring man who had come to him; but he took the poor man's lamb and prepared it for the man who had come to him."*
—2 Samuel 12:1–4

David listened to the prophet and then erupted in indignation at the obvious unfairness of the situation, saying, *"As the LORD lives, the man who has done this shall surely die! And he shall restore fourfold for the lamb, because he did this thing and because he had no pity"* (2 Samuel 12:5–6).

And then, in verse 7, the prophet utters some of the most famous, convicting words ever spoken, as he points at King David and declares, *"You are the man!"*

> *God confronts sin and also declares consequences.*

With that brief pronouncement, Nathan nailed David to the wall. He started off by telling David a story, knowing full well what the king's response would be, and then he pointed out that David was guilty of the very thing for which he had condemned the man in the story.

Now that he had the king's attention, Nathan went on to deliver his message from the Lord:

> *Thus says the LORD God of Israel: "I anointed you king over Israel, and I delivered you from the hand of Saul. I gave you your master's house and your master's wives into your keeping, and gave you the house of Israel and Judah. And if that had been too little, I also would have given you much more! Why have you despised the commandment of the LORD, to do evil in His sight? You have killed Uriah the Hittite with the sword; you have taken his wife to be your wife, and have killed him with the sword of the people of Ammon. Now therefore, the sword shall never depart from your house, because you*

*have despised Me, and have taken the wife of Uriah the
Hittite to be your wife." Thus says the LORD: "Behold, I
will raise up adversity against you from your own house;
and I will take your wives before your eyes and give them
to your neighbor, and he shall lie with your wives in the
sight of this sun. For you did it secretly, but I will do this
thing before all Israel, before the sun."*
—2 Samuel 12:7–12

God's pronouncement of David's sin was not gentle or halfhearted;
it never is. God confronts sin and calls it what it is. He also
declares consequences for our behavior—in David's case, major
consequences for major sin—consequences that impacted the
lives of others, as sin always does. But always, the purpose of
God's confronting us with our sin is to bring about confession,
repentance, and restoration of relationship.

David responded accordingly: *"I have sinned against the
LORD"* (2 Samuel 12:13). And immediately upon his confession,
which contained no excuses or sidestepping of responsibility or
guilt, Nathan pronounced God's forgiveness:

*"The LORD also has put away your sin; you shall not
die. However, because by this deed you have given
great occasion to the enemies of the LORD to blaspheme,
the child also who is born to you shall surely die."*
—2 Samuel 12:13–14

And then the prophet left.

In one visit from a man sent by God, the king's sin was exposed;
he confessed and repented; judgment and mercy were pronounced;
forgiveness and restoration were given and received.

The relationship between God and David was renewed—but
what about the relationship between David and Bathsheba? How
could the king ever make it right with her, especially since part of
the judgment for his sin would be the death of the child conceived
by his unlawful sexual relations with her?

There is a reason that David is often referred to as "a man after God's heart." Though he committed horrific sin—adultery and murder—when God confronted and convicted him, David immediately humbled himself, confessed his sin, and took full responsibility for it. And if he did so with God, we can safely assume that he also did so with Bathsheba.

No doubt at last recognizing the depth of his sin against this woman who was now his wife, it is easy to imagine him going to her and, in complete humility, begging her forgiveness. In addition, we know that David, after his confrontation by Nathan, penned the famous confessional that is Psalm 51:

*The psalm portrays David's desire to make things right.*

> *"Have mercy upon me, O God, according to Your lovingkindness; according to the multitude of Your tender mercies, blot out my transgressions. Wash me thoroughly from my iniquity, and cleanse me from my sin. For I acknowledge my transgressions, and my sin is always before me. Against You, You only, have I sinned, and done this evil in Your sight."*
> —Psalm 51:1–4

Not only do the contrite words of this psalm express to God David's depth of repentance, but it also shows his willingness to publicly declare his sin and exonerate Bathsheba. Though she isn't directly mentioned in the psalm, its timing, as well as the fact that David gave it to the chief musician to be used in public worship, clearly portrays David's desire to make things right with the woman he had so wronged.

Apparently it worked, as we shall see in the next section, for their relationship in the latter years was indeed a positive one.

## KING SOLOMON'S MOTHER

Though 1 Chronicles 3:5 tells us that David and Bathsheba went on to have four sons after their first baby died, it seems that

Solomon was Bathsheba's favorite, as he is the one Bathsheba lobbied for to be David's successor. We read that Nathan the prophet is again active in David and Bathsheba's lives (1 Kings 1). With King David quite old and nearly on his death bed, his son Adonijah moves to take over the kingdom. Nathan warns Bathsheba about it, telling her that if she doesn't intervene with David and convince him to crown Solomon as his successor before Adonijah completes his scheme, then both Solomon and Bathsheba will undoubtedly be killed.

Bathsheba heeds Nathan's warning and goes to David, reminding him of his promise to make Solomon king after him. She then tells him of Adonijah's actions and implores him to act quickly so that she and Solomon will be spared.

Before she has even finished speaking, Nathan comes to David and confirms Bathsheba's words regarding Adonijah, asking the king if it is his wish that Adonijah take over the throne.

In response, David swears to Bathsheba that he will do whatever is necessary to assure that Solomon becomes king—and then he follows through.

With Solomon safely ensconced as the ruling sovereign of Israel, even after David's death Bathsheba's position in the palace is assured, and her relationship with her son Solomon continues to be one of mutual affection and respect. This truth is evidenced when Adonijah, the son of Haggith as well as the son who tried to steal the throne, approaches Bathsheba to ask for a favor, indicating that he recognized her influence with King Solomon.

The favor he asked of her, however, was no small or innocent thing; it was, instead, another attempt to steal the throne. Whether or not Bathsheba realized this is uncertain, though if she did, she played along quite skillfully.

A young woman named Abishag, who had been David's nurse and companion before he died, was unmarried; Adonijah asked Bathsheba to request permission from Solomon to marry the king's former nurse. Bathsheba agreed to do so.

Now if Bathsheba were politically naive—which seems unlikely, since she had lived in the palace for many years—then she pressed ahead with the favor to Adonijah strictly because she was a nice lady who saw no reason not to convey this request to King Solomon. However, if she understood the implications of Adonijah's request, then she also understood the consequences that would likely result when Solomon heard what Adonijah wanted.

This was more than a simple request for a young woman's hand in marriage, for Abishag, though she had never had sexual relations with David, was technically his concubine. Requesting her as a wife exposed Adonijah for what he was—a traitor, still bent on taking over the kingdom.

Solomon had pardoned him once; he wouldn't do it again. Adonijah was put to death, and his threat of future rebellion died with him.

Yes, King Solomon had refused the request conveyed to him by his mother, but it wasn't because he didn't love or respect her. He denied the request because he recognized the evil intentions behind it. He also understood that his half-brother had approached Solomon through his mother because Adonijah recognized the close relationship the two of them had and thought that was his best chance for getting his request granted.

Of course, with or without Bathsheba's knowledge of the likely outcome, Adonijah's plan failed. But once again we see that not only was Solomon Bathsheba's favorite son, as she lobbied with the king to make Solomon his successor, but Bathsheba was also highly regarded by Solomon—so much so that some believe Solomon may have written Proverbs 31 in her honor.

*"Walk by faith, not by feelings—*
*your prayers cling, and so does God."*
—Judy Dippel, author

## Something to Think About/
## Enter in Your Journal:

1. Though you may not relate to Bathsheba as a woman who became both the wife and mother of a king, what shameful and/or heartbreaking incidents can you think of in your life that would enable you to relate to her as a violated woman or one who grieves the loss of a loved one?

2. Keeping in mind the depth of betrayal and humiliation Bathsheba must have felt at the hands of King David, describe the process you think she may have gone through that eventually enabled her to forgive and even love him. How can that process help you deal with some forgiveness issues in your own life?

3. Describe from Bathsheba's point of view what you see as the most significant elements of redemption and restoration in this story. How do these elements encourage you in situations in your own life?

*"Youth fades; love droops; the leaves of friendship fall.*
*A mother's secret hope outlives them all."*
—**Oliver Wendell Holmes Sr., physician, poet**

## A Mother's Prayer:

*Father, thank You that though You are a righteous God of judgment and there are consequences for our sins, You are also a God of mercy and grace. You rejoice in redeeming and restoring that which is lost—whether through our own sin or someone else's. Lord, help me now to place those broken relationships, those consequences of sin, and those painful memories in Your loving hands, believing You to redeem them as only You can—in Your time and for Your glory. I ask it in Jesus's wonderful name. Amen.*

*"Because I am a mother,*
*I hold God's greatest prize. And He expects*
*great things of me with a task of such a size."*
—**Grace Atkins, poet**

"The media tells single mothers we are raising ax murderers. But neither we nor our children are statistics. Thus, we must listen to the Lord and draw on our own God-given strength. We can walk this path and we can arrive at the finish line—not only as survivors but as victors."

—Sandra Aldrich, author

# CHAPTER 9

# The Widow of Zarephath: Generous to the End

*But I tell you truly, many widows were in Israel in the days of Elijah, when the heaven was shut up three years and six months, and there was a great famine throughout all the land; but to none of them was Elijah sent except to Zarephath, in the region of Sidon, to a woman who was a widow.*
—Luke 4:25–26

SUGGESTED SCRIPTURE READINGS:
1 Kings 16:29–34; 17; Luke 4:25–26

If we live in an economic situation where we and our children always have enough to eat, we should realize that we are blessed. It hasn't always been so throughout history, nor is it like that in parts of our present-day world. Daily, mothers in certain countries, communities, and cultures suffer need or even watch their children waste away from lack of nourishment, a tragedy so heartbreaking it is nearly beyond our imagining. So it was during the time of the prophet Elijah and his encounter with the widow of Zarephath.

This poor, destitute woman had already lost her husband, and in a time when there was a widespread famine in the land, that loss only compounded her difficulties. As far as we know from the biblical account, she had only one son, and he was apparently too young to provide for her, as an older son would automatically do in that culture.

*Evil that was present in the land gave reason for God's long and widespread curse of famine.*

The care and feeding of herself and her only child fell on her shoulders, shoulders that quickly bowed under the weight of a responsibility far too great for her to bear. When we are introduced to her in 1 Kings, she is in dire straits indeed.

❖ ❖ ❖

Though this widow and her son aren't mentioned until the 17th chapter of 1 Kings, the groundwork for her story and its relevance to us today is laid in the previous chapter, where we read of Ahab, the king who was in power at the time.

> *Now Ahab the son of Omri did evil in the sight of the LORD, more than all who were before him. And it came to pass, as though it had been a trivial thing for him to walk in the sins of Jeroboam the son of Nebat, that he took as wife Jezebel the daughter of Ethbaal, king of the Sidonians; and he went and served Baal and worshiped him.*
> —1 Kings 16:30–31

These verses, as well as others that precede the telling of the widow's story, paint a picture of the evil that was present in the land, and give reason for God's long and widespread curse of

Mothers of the Bible Speak to Mothers of Today

famine. It is in this life-threatening setting and sinful culture that we first meet the widow of Zarephath.

## CHALLENGED BY A PROPHET

We know little about this woman's life other than the fact that her husband had died, since she is called a widow, she had one son, and she lived in Phoenicia at Zarephath, about eight miles south of Sidon on the road to Tyre. This little bit of information, however, gives us enough background to get a clear picture of what her life must have been like.

First, she lived at a time and in a culture when a woman without a husband to protect and provide for her had a very difficult life. Widows depended on their children, particularly their sons, to care for them. Since only one child is mentioned in the story, and he a son too young to care for her, this particular woman had it even harder than most.

To compound the issue, there was a great famine in the land, brought on by a drought that, by the time of our story, had already continued for approximately two and a half years. Food was scarce, even for families whose husbands and fathers were still living. The widow's hardship was therefore quite easy to understand.

There is another factor that is interesting to note at this point, which is that the evil Queen Jezebel, who hated God and His faithful prophet Elijah, was also from the same home territory. Ironically, then, the prophet, who was running for his life from a queen who was originally from the same home turf, now goes to that very area to find a starving widow and her son who, according to God's instructions, will feed Elijah and keep him alive until the drought ends.

Prior to going to Zarephath, Elijah had already confronted King Ahab and declared to him God's promise that *"there shall not be dew nor rain these years, except at my word"* (1 Kings 17:1). Immediately following his pronouncement of the drought, Elijah received this word of direction from God:

> *"Get away from here and turn eastward, and hide by the Brook Cherith, which flows into the Jordan. And it will be that you shall drink from the brook, and I have commanded the ravens to feed you there."*
> —1 Kings 17:3–4

In response:

> *[Elijah] "went and did according to the word of the LORD, for he went and stayed by the Brook Cherith, which flows into the Jordan. The ravens brought him bread and meat in the morning, and bread and meat in the evening; and he drank from the brook.*
> —1 Kings 17:5–6

Eventually, however, *"the brook dried up, because there had been no rain in the land"* (1 Kings 17:7). At that point God again spoke to Elijah, directing him to a different source of divinely ordained provision: *"Arise, go to Zarephath, which belongs to Sidon, and dwell there. See, I have commanded a widow there to provide for you"* (1 Kings 17:9).

It is at this point that God introduces Elijah to the widow and he presents to her his first request: *"Please bring me a little water in a cup, that I may drink"* (1 Kings 17:10).

On the surface, this seems like a light request, but for the widow, it was more than that. The Scripture tells us that when Elijah first laid eyes on the widow, she was at the gate of the city, gathering sticks. What the Scripture doesn't tell us is what the widow looked like, though we begin to get a picture in our minds as we read on through the next verses.

Verse 11 tells us that the widow heeded Elijah's request and went to get him a drink of water, though we aren't quite sure why she did so. Did it possibly have anything to do with the fact that she recognized him as a prophet of God? Elijah was probably dressed in a coarse garment of camel's hair and wearing the mantle that signified his prophetic calling. Though the widow, as the vast majority of Zarephath's citizens, did not worship the God of Israel, she was undoubtedly aware of Him and may have recognized His followers. Perhaps, too, God opened her eyes to see that Elijah was a prophet of God, a man she should listen to and obey. Whatever the reason, she honored Elijah's request and interrupted her immediate task of gathering sticks in order to fetch him a drink.

*She scarcely had enough for one last meal.*

However, verse 11 then goes on to say that while she was on the way to get a drink for Elijah, he called out to her with yet another request: *"Please bring me a morsel of bread in your hand."* Now it was one thing to stop what she was doing and get some water for this foreign prophet; it was quite another to bring him food, since she scarcely had enough for one last meal for herself and her son. Her answer to the prophet in verse 12 clearly outlines how desperate her situation truly was:

> *"As the LORD your God lives, I do not have bread, only a handful of flour in a bin, and a little oil in a jar; and see, I am gathering a couple of sticks that I may go in and prepare it for myself and my son, that we may eat it, and die."*

This woman wasn't just out performing a daily task; she was gathering sticks in order to build a fire and use the last of her meager rations to make a meal for herself and her son. After that, she had resigned herself and her son to accept the fate that awaited them.

This statement of hers gives us a fairly clear idea of how she must have appeared to the prophet when first he saw her at the city gates. No doubt she walked with a stoop, long-since having lost any spring in her step—perhaps having buried it in the grave with her husband. That her raggedy clothes hung on her emaciated frame could be a given, and the look of hopelessness on her face must have been recognizable at first glance.

Yet Elijah called out to her, first for water and then for food. As difficult as the times were for everyone in that drought- and famine-stricken land, it would seem that a starving widow would not be the prophet's first choice when it came to obtaining the sustenance he needed to survive. But God had no doubt spotlighted that widow and assured Elijah that this was the very woman God had *"commanded"* (1 Kings 17:9) to provide for Elijah.

And so Elijah threw down the challenge. Upon the widow's explanation of her desperate predicament, Elijah responded with these words:

> *"Do not fear; go and do as you have said, but make me a small cake from it first, and bring it to me; and afterward make some for yourself and your son. For thus says the LORD God of Israel: 'The bin of flour shall not be used up, nor shall the jar of oil run dry, until the day the LORD sends rain on the earth.'"*
> —1 Kings 17:13–14

Those of us who are blessed to live in areas where food is usually more than plentiful are accustomed to giving out of our abundance. Unlike others who live in less bounteous situations, we may not have been asked to give out of our need or our poverty. It is easy to loan or give a couple of eggs to a neighbor when we know we have another dozen safely tucked away in the refrigerator; it is quite another challenge altogether if the neighbor asks to borrow our last two eggs—and we have no prospect of getting any more.

That's the situation the widow was in, with the prophet asking for the last meal she had, the food she planned to fix for her son and herself before starvation finished them off. But Elijah didn't ask for the food in his name; he asked for it in the name of the Lord God of Israel by promising that if the widow would accept this challenge and obey God's command, He would provide for her and her son until the drought ended.

Now she may not have been a believer or worshiper of this God of Israel, but she had obviously heard about Him, and somehow knew she was in the presence of one of His prophets. As a result, she took a giant leap of faith and obeyed, going home to fix that last meal and then presenting it to the prophet, though her stomach no doubt growled and her mouth salivated as she watched him eat it. Worse yet, her heart ached to think she had deprived her beloved son of his last meal on earth—unless this God of Israel came through as promised.

And isn't that the bottom line? Isn't that exactly where God wants us? Not just giving a pittance out of our abundance, but recognizing that all is His—everything—and He has a right to ask us for it at any time. In fact, at some point in each of our lives, if we call ourselves followers of the one true God, He will certainly confront us and demand that we give up that which is most precious to us—as He did with the widow of Zarephath, as He did with Abraham when He told the patriarch to sacrifice his only son Isaac, as He did with Esther when her uncle challenged her to risk her life by intervening with the king on behalf of the Jewish people.

The widow of Zarephath responded honorably and with faith, obeying God and giving up the last of her worldly provision; in return, God honored His promise and provided for her and her son—as well as Elijah the prophet—by ensuring just enough flour and oil each day to keep all three of them alive and well until rain once more poured down upon the earth.

*God's daily provision was confirmation of faithfulness and trustworthiness.*

## RESTORED BY PRAYER

God's daily provision of flour and oil for the widow and her son and Elijah was a powerful confirmation of the faithfulness of God and the absolute trustworthiness of His promises. But the widow was new to this faith-walk, and like so many of us who have witnessed God's miraculous provision in our lives, she faltered when her faith was tested.

As mothers we can especially relate to this woman's shaky faith, particularly because her test came in relation to her son. Is there anything more difficult than trusting God—completely, 100 percent, no-holds-barred—when it comes to our children? It isn't nearly so difficult to yield to God and trust Him when we are the only ones affected. But our offspring? Now that's another story altogether.

And yet, throughout the Bible, we see stories of both mothers and fathers who are tested to the point of giving up their children to God. Abraham, as mentioned earlier, had to do so with Isaac when he took him up to the mountain to offer him as a sacrifice. Jochebed placed baby Moses in a basket and hid him in the reeds of the river, trusting God to protect and deliver him. Hannah took the son she had prayed for and gave him over to Eli the priest to raise him at the tabernacle. And can there be any greater example of a mother being forced to trust God for the life of her child than Mary of Nazareth?

This poor widow, who had lost everything and had only recently come to faith in the one true God, seemed to have regained her footing and assurance in life when suddenly the rug was pulled out from under her. In one fell swoop, her faith was dashed and her heart broken when, according to 1 Kings 17:17:

> *Now it happened after these things [God's miraculous provision for the widow and her son and Elijah] that the son of the woman who owned the house became sick. And his sickness was so serious that there was no breath left in him.*

In other words, the widow's son became seriously ill and died, leaving this woman not only grief-stricken but guilt-stricken as well. Though she had become a follower of the God of Israel, she apparently hadn't come to grips with the forgiveness and restoration God had granted to her because she may have assumed her son's death was God's punishment upon her for her pagan living prior to her conversion.

*That's the message of Calvary: the punishment has already been meted out.*

Isn't that something we've all wrestled with at times? If we've accepted Jesus as our Savior, we know He has forgiven us and we've been adopted into God's family. We are His sons and daughters for all eternity, and nothing or no one can change that because God's promises are true and forever. And yet....

Aren't there times when the devil—or our own self-absorbed

imaginations—tempts us to believe that something bad has happened to us as a result of some former sin? No matter that the sin is "under the blood," paid for by the death and resurrection of the very Son of God; we so easily fall into the trap of thinking we have somehow brought about—or earned—God's punishment for sins committed long ago. Do we deserve such punishment? Of course! But that's the message of Calvary: the punishment has already been meted out. Jesus took our punishment for us. If we fall into the trap of thinking we can "earn" punishment for our bad behavior, then we can just as easily fall into the trap of thinking we can "earn" God's forgiveness or love or salvation. Apparently this was a lesson the widow of Zarephath had to learn as well.

When the widow's son died, she confronted Elijah with these words: *"What have I to do with you, O man of God? Have you come to me to bring my sin to remembrance, and to kill my son?"* (1 Kings 17:18). In other words, she asked him if he had come to her house only to draw God's attention to her so He would be reminded of her sinful life and punish her by killing her son.

Though this may sound like faulty logic, this was a woman who had lived in a pagan culture her entire life until the prophet came to stay at her home and her eyes were opened to the truth. But she was still quite new in her faith, and when her only son's life had seemingly been taken from her, it's understandable that she might come to such a conclusion.

Elijah, however, didn't even respond to her question. He simply said, *"Give me your son"* (1 Kings 17:19). Then he took the boy to the upper room where the prophet stayed, and prayed until God restored the child's life. The prophet then *"took the child and brought him down from the upper room into the house, and gave him to his mother"* (1 Kings 17:23), and he said to her in that same verse, *"See, your son lives!"*

Even as Mary of Nazareth rejoiced at her Son's resurrection centuries later, so the widow of Zarephath rejoiced that this son had been restored to her as well. Her words to Elijah reveal the new depth of her faith after that incident: *"Now by this I know that you are a man of God, and that the word of the LORD in your mouth is the truth"* (1 Kings 17:24).

The widow of Zarephath now knew without a doubt that when God spoke a word, it would come to pass, regardless of the circumstances. Her living, breathing son was all the proof she would ever need to remind her of God's faithfulness.

## REMEMBERED BY JESUS

Not everyone who is mentioned in the Old Testament is again mentioned in the New Testament, specifically by Jesus Himself, but the widow of Zarephath is one of the few. When Jesus was speaking in the synagogue in His own hometown, He confronted His neighbors—the very ones who had seen Him grow up and who knew Him and His family well—and pointed out their lack of faith, using the widow of Zarephath as an example.

Wouldn't it have been nice if Jesus had named the woman when referring to her? Surely He knew her name, though it was never mentioned in the 1 Kings account. Then again, perhaps He didn't for that very reason—to keep the focus off the woman and on God who was her faithful Provider. His purpose for pointing

*God sometimes uses the least likely among us to exhibit His greatness.*

out this poverty-stricken widow wasn't to glorify or praise her, but to point out that God sometimes uses the least likely among us to exhibit His greatness. Here is how Jesus told the story:

> *"Assuredly, I say to you, no prophet is accepted in his own country. But I tell you truly, many widows were in Israel in the days of Elijah, when the heaven was shut up three years and six months, and there was a great famine throughout all the land; but to none of them was Elijah sent except to Zarephath, in the region of Sidon, to a woman who was a widow. And many lepers were in Israel in the time of Elisha the prophet, and none of them was cleansed except Naaman the Syrian."*
> —Luke 4:24–28

Not only did Jesus point out that God had used a poor widow from a pagan culture to sustain His prophet Elijah, but Jesus also gave the example of Naaman, another pagan from Syria, whom God healed of leprosy rather than any of the many lepers in Israel.

These examples were not well received by Jesus's listeners, for verses 28 or 29 tell us:

> *All those in the synagogue, when they heard these things, were filled with wrath, and rose up and thrust Him out of the city; and they led Him to the brow of the hill on which their city was built, that they might throw Him down over the cliff.*

A bit of an extreme reaction, to say the least! It seems Jesus's listeners were none too pleased at having their lack of faith pointed out to them, along with the example of God having used sinners or pagans to accomplish His purposes. Yet Jesus was speaking these words in love, using His examples to try to help these people understand who He was and why it was so important for them to listen to and follow Him.

Some did, of course. Like the widow of Zarephath, they turned from their former lives and joined themselves to the one true God. Others, however, refused to believe, choosing instead to continue in their own way, following their own gods and their own desires. The outcome was, as Jesus knew it would be, tragic.

Isn't it amazing how words from Jesus, words that confront us right where we are, words that offer hope and forgiveness and eternal life, can evoke a flicker of faith in some but stoke the fires of hatred in others? That's what happened when Jesus brought to His listeners' remembrance the familiar story of the widow of Zarephath, who was so mightily used to preserve the life of God's prophet Elijah. Some, no doubt, stored up His words and pondered them, possibly even praying over them, while others became infuriated and tried to kill the Source of those words. Jesus, however, could not be killed until it was time for Him to willingly lay down His life of His own accord. Since this was not the time, verse 30 pulls together this confrontational scene with these words: *"Then passing through the midst of them, He went His way."*

The angry mob thought they had Jesus on the ropes—on the edge of a cliff, actually—but He calmly walked right through the middle of them and went on His way.

Neither circumstances or people, nor problems or demons, can stop the will of God when He has purposed to do something. In the story of the widow of Zarephath, God purposed to care for the prophet Elijah, first through the provisions of a brook and ravens, then through a continual supply of flour and oil at a poverty-stricken widow's home. He had also purposed to bring a poor widow woman and her son to faith in Him, and not even a pagan background or culture, a powerful king or an evil queen, or the death of a son could prevent those purposes from being fulfilled.

Jesus honored this widow of Zarephath by reminding His listeners of how God had used her, a woman who would otherwise be a highly unlikely heroine for any story. And, for the most part, doesn't that describe all of us? Don't we all feel inadequate and unqualified for any sort of notoriety or honor bestowed upon us, particularly by God Himself?

But that's what makes the story of this widow and her son so personal. She was down to nothing—her last can of soup but no power to run the can opener; her last loaf of bread with nothing but a stale crust left in the bag; her last piece of cheese, covered with mold. It was about as bad as it gets. Then God shows up and says, "Give it to Me. All of it. What little you have left, hand it over. I want to use it for something. And then I'll take care of you. I'll feed you and your son, every day, for as long as you have need."

When you really believe that God is good and faithful and keeps His word, that sounds like a great deal, doesn't it? But when you've never met God, never tested Him to see if He's who and what He claims to be, it's a little bit tougher to hand over that last paltry meal. Though you know it can't sustain you forever, it's yours—and it's all you've got. You're not being asked to give out of your abundance; you're being asked to give it all, and to trust God for everything.

That's what happened to the widow of Zarephath, and she responded well. A pagan woman in a pagan land—the same city from which the evil Queen Jezebel hailed—responded better than many who had been born and raised in the Jewish faith. Jesus wanted His listeners to understand that God's love and forgiveness, as well as His faithfulness and provision, were available for all who would believe and trust Him, and so He used the example of a poor widow and her son to make His point.

*"An abundance of money is not a requirement for being a good mother; the poorest of mothers often raise the richest of children."*
**—Dayle Shockley, author**

1. What times have you experienced in your own life when you felt you were down to your last can of soup or moldy piece of cheese? Can you think of miraculous ways God may have intervened to meet your needs and carry you through those times?

2. Consider those times in your life when you've been pressed to give when you felt there was nothing to spare. How did you react? Are you pleased with the way you handled those times? If not, how would you handle them differently now?

3. In relation to the way the widow reacted when her son died, can you think of instances in your own faith walk when you believe you failed God by reacting negatively and doubting Him? What have you learned since that time that might change the way you would deal with those same situations now?

*"Mother love is the fuel that enables a normal human being to do the impossible."*
**—Marion C. Garretty, author**

## A Mother's Prayer:

*Father God, thank You that You use those who are most unlikely or unqualified to be heroes in the faith—because that means You can use me. Forgive me, Lord, for those many times I have failed to trust You to provide for my needs, despite Your previous faithfulness and Your continued promises. Help me, Father, to remember the widow of Zarephath and her willingness to trust You with everything. May I, too, have that sort of faith, not in my own abilities or worthiness, but in Yours. Thank You, Lord, in Jesus's name. Amen.*

*"My mother had a slender, small body, but a large heart—a heart so large that everybody's joys found welcome in it, and hospitable accommodation."*
**—Mark Twain (Samuel Langhorne Clemens), author, humorist**

*"Prayer is a covering for the child and a comfort for the mother."*

—Dolley Carlson, author

# CHAPTER 10

# Elizabeth: A Willing Sacrifice

*And they [Zacharias and Elizabeth] were both righteous before God, walking in all the commandments and ordinances of the Lord blameless. But they had no child, because Elizabeth was barren, and they were both well advanced in years.*
—Luke 1:6–7

SUGGESTED SCRIPTURE READINGS:
Luke 1; Matthew 11:11

Though the telling of Elizabeth's life is limited almost completely to one chapter of the Bible, there is much we can learn about her in those 80 verses—and much we can use as a guideline in our own lives as wives, mothers, and daughters of our heavenly Father.

There is the obvious, of course, in that Elizabeth had passed what would be considered her childbearing years and yet had not known the joys of motherhood. In a culture where motherhood was esteemed above nearly any other attribute of womanhood, this was no easy condition to bear. And yet, we see no evidence that she had become jealous or bitter or self-serving. Her characteristics, in fact, seem to be just the opposite, with humility, patience, and self-sacrifice being at the top of the list.

As other barren women mentioned in the Scriptures, including the great Hebrew matriarch Sarah, Elizabeth no doubt longed for a child. Had she come to the age of giving up all hope? Possibly. But in Luke 1:37, the angel Gabriel speaks to Mary of Nazareth. After telling Mary that her older cousin Elizabeth was at last expecting a child, Gabriel captures the story of Elizabeth, wife of Zacharias, mother of John the Baptist, and aunt of Jesus Himself: *"For with God nothing will be impossible."* That verse epitomizes Elizabeth's conceiving and bearing of her son, John, as well as her ability to humbly and honorably serve the God of her fathers, regardless of the circumstances, and it speaks to us of the hope God has for all of us.

❖ ❖ ❖

The first thing we learn about Elizabeth in Luke 1:5 is that she is the wife of a priest named Zacharias and that she herself was descended from the Aaronic, or priestly, tribe of Israel. And so we know that both Elizabeth and Zacharias, the parents of John the Baptist, the cousin and forerunner of the Messiah, were well schooled in the Scriptures. We also know that they were more than "readers" of the Scriptures; they were "doers" as well, for verse 6 tells us *"they were both righteous before God, walking in all the commandments and ordinances of the Lord blameless."*

A godly couple with a godly heritage—and yet, according to verse 7, *"they had no child, because Elizabeth was barren, and they were both well advanced in years."* They were born in the right place, to the right families, with the right bloodlines, and they did their best to do all the right things—and still they suffered a serious lack in their lives. For any of us who have suffered similar situations—some for years, as did Zacharias and Elizabeth—life just doesn't seem fair, whether we have all the right pedigrees or not. And yet Elizabeth continued to be the honorable, humble woman she no doubt was when she was young and still dreaming of being a mother one day.

How did she do it? And how can her faithfulness help us to do likewise? Perhaps a closer look at this older cousin of the young virgin, Mary of Nazareth, will give us insight into how we too can have a humble heart, free of bitterness and envy, regardless of unfulfilled longings and seeming inequities.

## HONORED AND BELOVED WIFE

Elizabeth is best known as John the Baptist's mother and Mary of Nazareth's cousin, but before either of those titles was true, Elizabeth was the wife of Zacharias, a priest who served at the Temple. Together they served God, blamelessly following *"all the commandments and ordinances of the Lord"* (Luke 1:6). Of course, we know that doesn't mean they were perfect, since no one but Jesus has ever walked upon this earth without sin. But they lived according to the Law of Moses, including the offering up of sacrifices when they did sin. They were obviously a godly couple, a shining example to others of how faithful Israelites should live, both as man and wife and as servants of the Most High God.

*They were obviously a shining example.*

We also know from verse 13 that Zacharias had actively been praying and interceding for his wife, beseeching God to give them a child, even in their old age, for the angel said to him, *"Do not be afraid, Zacharias, for your prayer is heard; and your wife Elizabeth will bear you a son."*

Zacharias was obviously familiar with the Scriptures and believed that the same God who allowed Sarah to conceive and bear a child in her nineties could do the same for Elizabeth, and so he faithfully prayed to that end. Later, after the birth of their son, before Zacharias regained his voice, it was Elizabeth who announced their son's name. When the townspeople questioned Elizabeth's choice, Zacharias confirmed it by writing *"His name is John"* on a tablet, thus releasing his tongue to speak once again, even as he affirmed his wife in the presence of others.

There is no indication that Elizabeth's barrenness ever caused a division between herself and Zacharias. They lived together as man and wife, and faithfully served God together—a priest married to a woman descended from the High Priest Aaron, brother of Moses the Lawgiver. Except for lack of a child, their marriage was no doubt a joyous and fulfilling union.

## HUMBLE AND JOYOUS MOTHER-TO-BE

At last, however, the home that had never known the patter of little feet or the thin wail of a newborn would now have reason to rejoice, to proclaim the announcement to the entire city, as the angel Gabriel declared to Mary only a few months before John's birth: *"For with God nothing will be impossible"* (Luke 1:37). The barren woman would be barren no more! She who had quietly but longingly looked on as her friends and relatives nursed their infants at their breast would now hold a son in her arms and do the same. The level of her joy is nearly impossible to comprehend—unless you too are a woman who has longed for a child, in which case the feeling of empty arms is only too real and close to home.

*The level of her joy is nearly impossible to comprehend.*

How did Elizabeth receive the news? Unlike Mary, who was personally visited by the angel Gabriel and given the news of her impending pregnancy firsthand, Elizabeth undoubtedly heard it from her husband. For it was to the priest Zacharias, as he served in the Temple, that the angelic messenger came.

It happened on a day when a large crowd of people were outside the Temple building, praying, and Zacharias *"was serving as priest before God in the order of his division, according to the custom of the priesthood"* that *"his lot fell to burn incense when he went into the temple of the Lord"* (Luke 1:8–9). In other words, as one of many priests who served at the Temple, it was Zacharias's turn to offer incense and pray to God. And while he was performing his duties as priest, *"an angel of the Lord appeared to him, standing on the right side of the altar of incense"* (Luke 1:11).

Naturally, Zacharias was afraid. Though he was a priest, prepared to serve in the Temple and regularly following the commandments and ordinances of God, he was not accustomed to having angels appear before his eyes. The angel, however, immediately spoke to allay his fears:

> *"Do not be afraid, Zacharias, for your prayer is heard; and your wife Elizabeth will bear you a son, and you shall call his name John. And you will have joy and gladness, and many will rejoice at his birth. For he will be great in the sight of the Lord, and shall drink neither wine nor strong drink. He will also be filled with the Holy Spirit, even from his mother's womb. And he will turn many of the children of Israel to the Lord their God. He will also go before Him in the spirit and power of Elijah, 'to turn the hearts of the fathers to the children,' and the disobedient to the wisdom of the just, to make ready a people prepared for the Lord."*
> —Luke 1:13-17

Wow, what a promise! Not only are Zacharias and Elizabeth going to conceive and bear a son in their old age, but God has promised to use this son mightily.

First the angel tells Zacharias not to be afraid but to rejoice because God has heard his prayer. That in itself is exciting news when you've been praying for years and nothing seems to be happening. But even as the years came and went, making the likelihood of answered prayer more and more improbable, Zacharias didn't give up. What a lesson to those of us who want to throw in the towel when our prayers aren't answered after a few weeks or even months.

Persevering in prayer is one of the toughest things any of us will ever do, but it is the very act that exhibits to God our faith in Him—in His ability to answer, His willingness to do so, His perfect timing and response. In all the years Zacharias prayed—and no doubt Elizabeth did as well—he certainly never expected the answer to come from the lips of an angel.

Isn't that another powerful lesson for us to learn about persevering in prayer? Not only is God in charge of the timing of His answer, but He will do so in His way, not ours—and often when we least expect it.

*Not only is God in charge of the timing of His answer, but He will do so in His way.*

The angel then tells Zacharias that his son will be *"great in the sight of the Lord, and shall drink neither wine nor strong drink"* (Luke 1:15). The angel's statement that their son will not drink *"wine nor strong drink"* may indicate that he, "like Samson, was to be a Nazirite, dedicated to God in the special way outlined in Numbers 6:1-21," according to David H. Stern's *Jewish New Testament Commentary*. Whether or not that was the case, it was obvious that John, like his parents before him, would be a believer in and a servant of the Most High God, and that had to be a pleasing announcement to Zacharias's ears.

The angel then went on to give an even more astounding prophecy: *"He will also be filled with the Holy Spirit, even from his mother's womb"* (Luke 1:15). This is a very important verse, not only because it foretells the source of John's power to do all the things he will do in his lifetime, but it also establishes that even before his birth, while he is yet in his mother's womb, John is an individual with personhood. Though some translations say he would be filled with the Holy Spirit *"from birth,"* others say *"from his mother's womb,"* a key distinction that is seemingly confirmed, according to Sue and Larry Richards's *Women of the Bible*, in verse 41, which says, *"And it happened, when Elizabeth heard the greeting of Mary, that the babe leaped in her womb; and Elizabeth was filled with the Holy Spirit."* God sent His Spirit to fill an unborn baby of great promise. It was that powerful infilling of John while still in his mother's womb that enabled and empowered him to become the man God had called him to be.

And that great truth applies to all of us. Unless we are born again and have God's Spirit dwelling within us, we can do virtually nothing except serve ourselves. John was called to serve God and others, and he needed God's Spirit within him to be able to fulfill that calling. We have been called to that same service, and therefore need God's Spirit within us as well.

Finally, the angel tells Zacharias of the great things John will accomplish and who it is he will come to serve and glorify:

> *"And he will turn many of the children of Israel to the Lord their God. He will also go before Him in the spirit and power of Elijah, 'to turn the hearts of the fathers to the children,' and the disobedient to the wisdom of the just, to make ready a people prepared for the Lord."*
> —Luke 1:16–17

John would not be the long-awaited Messiah, but he would be the one to go ahead of that Messiah, to call people to repentance, to turn their hearts back to God, and to spotlight the Messiah in their midst.

What an honor! And this was the announcement that Zacharias would carry home to Elizabeth—though at that point, because of his weak faith, he could no longer speak. For when the angel had completed making this great announcement to Zacharias, pointing out to him that it would be God's Spirit that would empower this miraculous event from start to finish, Zacharias expressed his doubts by saying, *"How shall I know this? For I am an old man, and my wife is well advanced in years"* (Luke 1:18). Zacharias may have been a priest, but he didn't get it! He actually thought he had to do his part in this prophesied miracle in and through his own strength. And so the angel closed the mouth of Zacharias until he could learn to speak in faith: *"You will be mute and not able to speak until the day these things take place, because you did not believe my words which will be fulfilled in their own time"* (Luke 1:20).

Aren't you glad God doesn't strike us mute each time we utter words of unbelief? I, for one, would spend a lot more time speechless! But that's exactly what happened to Zacharias, and so he progressed through Elizabeth's conception and pregnancy without speaking a word. Somehow, however, he was able to convey to his wife the glorious promise of God, and our humble and honorable heroine received the news with joy. At last, she was to have a child of her own!

Yet, as thrilled and excited as she was, Elizabeth knew her child would be the forerunner to the Messiah, not the Messiah Himself. What she didn't know when Zacharias first told her of the impending birth was that her own cousin—a young virgin named Mary from the city of Nazareth—would be the one to bear that promised Messiah.

After Mary had her own angelic visit, she decided to make a trip to visit her older cousin Elizabeth. If anyone would understand about a miraculous pregnancy, Mary undoubtedly reasoned, it would be Elizabeth. And, of course, she was right.

From the moment Elizabeth heard Mary's voice, the elder cousin understood more than she had ever dreamed possible, as verses 41–45 so clearly illustrate.

> *And it happened, when Elizabeth heard the greeting of Mary, that the babe leaped in her womb; and Elizabeth was filled with the Holy Spirit. Then she spoke out with a loud voice and said, "Blessed are you among women, and blessed is the fruit of your womb! But why is this granted to me, that the mother of my Lord should come to me? For indeed, as soon as the voice of your greeting sounded in my ears, the babe leaped in my womb for joy. Blessed is she who believed, for there will be a fulfillment of those things which were told her from the Lord."*

Elizabeth, who by then had spent countless hours pondering the prophetic proclamation spoken over her own son, John, suddenly grasped the identity of the Messiah her son would serve—the Son of her cousin Mary! How did she know this? The minute Mary spoke a word of greeting to Elizabeth, John the Baptist—as yet an unborn infant—leaped within his mother's womb. Immediately afterward, Elizabeth was filled with the Holy Spirit, who revealed the truth to her as she spoke forth her words of prophetic blessing.

Elizabeth's humility is beautifully illustrated in her words to Mary: *"But why is this granted to me, that the mother of my Lord should come to me?"* In other words, who am I that the mother of the long-awaited Messiah would visit me? That Mary would come to Elizabeth's home was not unusual; they were, after all, cousins. But that the woman who was pregnant with the Messiah would deign to visit her was more than Elizabeth could fathom.

*Two women, so far apart in age yet so close in destiny, shared their hearts.*

Together, these two women, so far apart in age yet so close in destiny, shared their hearts and their dreams, their joys and their fears, as they looked forward to holding in their arms the babies that God had divinely placed within them. But even as they planned and dreamed, did these two expectant mothers ever suspect the swords of sorrow that would one day pierce their hearts?

## WILLING AND OBEDIENT DAUGHTER

The Bible tells us that when *"Elizabeth's full time came for her to be delivered...she brought forth a son"* (Luke 1:57). What an event that must have been! Anytime a child, particularly a son, was born in that time and culture, it was cause for celebration. Life was considered sacred, and the birth of a healthy new life was an exciting occurrence, so it's no surprise that the good news spread quickly, and her relatives and neighbors *"rejoiced with her"* (Luke 1:58). Then, as was the custom, on the eighth day they took the baby to the Temple for his *B'rit-milah*, or circumcision and official naming ceremony.

This action by Zacharias and Elizabeth was in keeping with what we learned about them earlier: *"And they were both righteous before God, walking in all the commandments and ordinances of the Lord blameless"* (Luke 1:6). According to the covenant God made with Abraham (see Genesis 17:10–14), circumcision was a requirement for all Jewish males, and it was to be done on the eighth day after birth (see Genesis 17:12 and Leviticus 12:3). It was at this same time that the son would receive his name, almost always the name of some close family member. As a result, those who had come to celebrate with Zacharias and Elizabeth assumed the baby's name would be Zacharias, but Elizabeth stunned them when she said otherwise: *"No; he shall be called John"* (Luke 1:60).

The people argued with her that there was no one in their family named John, but when Elizabeth wouldn't yield to their arguments, the people turned to Zacharias and *"made signs to his father—what he would have him called"* (Luke 1:62).

Zacharias, who was still mute, got a tablet and wrote these words, affirming his wife and honoring the angelic instructions he had received months earlier: *"His name is John"* (Luke 1:63).

At that instant, the Bible tells us, *"his mouth was opened and his tongue loosed, and he spoke, praising God"* (Luke 1:64). As a result:

*Fear came on all who dwelt around them; and all these sayings were discussed throughout all the hill country of Judea. And all those who heard them kept them in their hearts, saying, "What kind of child will this be?" And the hand of the Lord was with him.*
—Luke 1:65–66

What a circumcision celebration that must have been! Elizabeth would certainly never forget it. Though she had believed God's word all along, as was obvious in her actions and words to that point, she had now seen her husband's speech restored, and she had to have known it was because he honored and believed God by defying tradition and obeying the angel's instruction to name the child John. News of such an event must have spread like wildfire, adding to the already existing stories of a miraculous conception and birth on the part of the elderly priest Zacharias and his previously barren wife, Elizabeth.

*He honored and believed God by defying tradition and obeying the angel's instruction.*

From that point on, all eyes were undoubtedly fixed on this little family. In a culture where people made it their business to know what was going on with the other people in their city or village, little went unnoticed when it came to a child born in such miraculous circumstances. And though we have no specific biblical accounts of a childhood friendship between John and Jesus, it may be safe to assume that one could have existed, and that it flourished as they grew older, although they lived miles apart.

In addition, we know from verse 66 that *"the hand of the Lord was with"* John and that *"the child grew and became strong in spirit, and was in the deserts till the day of his manifestation to Israel"* (Luke 1:80). We also know that his father, Zacharias, after having his speech restored, made a powerful, prophetic proclamation about his son's life—and that Elizabeth must have been absorbing every word that he spoke, storing them in her heart for future reference:

*"Blessed is the Lord God of Israel, for He has visited and redeemed His people, and has raised up a horn of salvation for us in the house of His servant David, as He spoke by the mouth of His holy prophets, who have been since the world began, that we should be saved from our enemies and from the hand of all who hate us, to perform the mercy promised to our fathers and to remember His holy covenant, the oath which He swore to our father Abraham: to grant us that we, being delivered from the hand of our enemies, might serve Him without fear, in holiness and righteousness before Him all the days of our life. And you, child, will be called the prophet of the Highest; for you will go before the face of the Lord to prepare His ways, to give knowledge of salvation to His people by the remission of their sins, through the tender mercy of our God, with which the Dayspring from on high has visited us; to give light to those who sit in darkness and the shadow of death, to guide our feet into the way of peace."*
—Luke 1:68–79

Even for a mother who had experienced her baby leaping in her womb at the sound of the Savior's mother's voice, these words of Zacharias must have been overwhelming. And yet, because she was first and foremost a humble and honorable daughter of God Himself, she was able to accept what she could understand and submit the rest to the Most High, knowing He loved her son, John, more than she or Zacharias ever could.

Was she a good mother, a devoted mother who raised a godly son? Jesus, years later during His earthly ministry, said this of Elizabeth and John: *"Assuredly, I say to you, among those born of women there has not risen one greater than John the Baptist"* (Matthew 11:11).

Elizabeth was a humble, honorable woman, who loved and served God, her husband, and her son. Did she often think of and pray for Jesus, even as she watched her beloved John grow as well? Though both sons would die at the hands of cruel and violent men, Elizabeth, like Mary, was sustained in the knowledge of God's perfect plan for all mankind—and the part they played in its unfolding.

*Elizabeth, like Mary, was sustained in the knowledge of God's perfect plan.*

*"I remember my mother's prayers and they have always followed me. They have clung to me all my life."*
**—Abraham Lincoln, US President**

## Something to Think About/
## Enter in Your Journal:

1. When you consider Elizabeth's "pedigree" of being descended from a priestly line and being married to a priest, how does that make you feel personally? If you can't relate to her on those lines, how do you feel knowing that despite those seemingly impeccable qualifications, Elizabeth still had to wait many years before receiving the desire of her heart?

2. Consider Elizabeth's response to Mary's visit: a) her baby's stunning reaction; b) her realization of what was going on in Mary's life; c) her humble and submissive words to a girl who was her younger cousin. What does all that speak to you in your own circumstances, and how can you incorporate it in a way that will help to fulfill God's purpose for your own life and others'?

3. Now put yourself in the place of Elizabeth as the years pass by and your son is a man, living the hermit-like life of a prophet and gaining as many enemies as friends and followers. How do you prepare yourself to release your child to God, whatever the outcome?

*"As your heart swells with love for your children, remember that it's God who placed it there—it's powerful!"*
—**Judy Dippel, author**

## A Mother's Prayer:

*Father, thank You that Your promises can be trusted to be fulfilled in Your time and in Your way. Thank You too that you know so much better than I what is best for me. When I pray to see the desires of my heart fulfilled, Lord, may it be done according to Your time and purposes, and in a way that will honor and glorify You. Give me an honorable and humble heart, like Elizabeth's, and help me to be grateful for whatever comes by way of Your divine purpose and plan. I ask it in Jesus's wonderful name. Amen.*

**"Mama exhorted her children at every opportunity to 'jump at de sun.' We might not land on the sun, but at least we would get off the ground."**
**—Zora Neale Hurston, author, anthropologist**

*"In the eyes of its mother every beetle is a gazelle."*

—African proverb

# CHAPTER 11

# The Canaanite Woman: Persevering in Prayer

*Then she came and worshiped Him, saying, "Lord, help me!" But He answered and said, "It is not good to take the children's bread and throw it to the little dogs." And she said, "Yes, Lord, yet even the little dogs eat the crumbs which fall from their masters' table." Then Jesus answered and said to her, "O woman, great is your faith! Let it be to you as you desire." And her daughter was healed from that very hour."*
—Matthew 15:25–28

SUGGESTED SCRIPTURE READINGS:
Matthew 15:21–28; Mark 7:24–30

The Syro-Phoenician woman. The Canaanite woman. The woman with no name. The woman with a demon-possessed daughter. The pagan woman with no particular claim to the Jewish Messiah....

That's the woman who came to Jesus, seeking help for her child—a woman with no direct right to do so, a woman much like you and me.

And yet Jesus helped her. He healed her daughter, and in the process, made an impact on a Gentile city for generations to come. What power and promise that message holds for us!

❖ ❖ ❖

This nameless woman, whose heart was grieved over her demon-possessed daughter, lived on the border of the Holy Land, on the northern frontier of Palestine, about three or more days' walk from Jerusalem. She was not a member of the Jewish faith, but rather a Greek and a pagan, a Gentile, though probably of Semitic stock, since Matthew called her "a woman of Canaan," referring to the ancient land of Canaan. Mark, however, referred to her as Syro-Phoenician because she lived in the country of Phoenicia, which belonged to Syria.

Regardless of her heritage or lack of "pedigree," she was a mother who dearly loved her child and had probably despaired of ever seeing her freed. And then she heard of Jesus, the so-called Jewish Prophet to whom many miracles were ascribed. Was it possible that He could—that He *would*—heal the daughter of a nameless Gentile who had no right even to ask?

There was only one way to find out....

## A DESPERATE MOTHER

The first thing this dear woman cried out when she approached Jesus was, *"Have mercy on me, O Lord, Son of David! My daughter is severely demon-possessed"* (Matthew 15:22). On the surface, this seemed to be a reasonable approach from a desperate woman, not unlike many He had received and answered before. Jesus, however, uncharacteristically ignored her. Verse 23, in fact, tells us *"He answered her not a word."* Why would Jesus do that? Nowhere else in the Gospels do we find Jesus turning away from a legitimate need. Why, then, would He completely ignore such a heartrending request from such an obviously needy individual?

The answer is found in Jesus's response to His disciples' urging to *"Send her away, for she cries out after us"* (Matthew 15:23). The woman was undoubtedly attracting attention and becoming an annoyance and embarrassment, and the disciples just wanted Jesus to grant her request, as He had so many others, and send her on her way. Their concern wasn't so much for the woman or her daughter, but rather for themselves. This was not a woman they wished to be associated with, and the sooner she was gone, the better.

> *The Lord Jesus, however, corrected their thinking.*

The Lord Jesus, however, corrected their thinking with one brief statement: *"I was not sent except to the lost sheep of the house of Israel"* (Matthew 15:24). In other words, He wasn't on an immediate mission to rescue the lost Gentiles, but rather the lost sheep of Israel. This wasn't so much an insult to the Gentiles in general or the Syro-Phoenician woman specifically, but rather a reminder to the many Jews who followed and listened to Him that it was they—despite their proper lineage and religious rules and regulations—who needed a Savior. Though His rescue mission would eventually extend to the Gentiles as well as to the Jews, Jesus wanted to make the immediate objects of His salvation message—the Jewish people—perfectly clear.

## A HUMBLE SERVANT

Was our heroine offended by the apparent rebuff of Jesus? If so, she certainly didn't show it. In fact, she responded in a most humble manner, changing her manner of approach and saying simply, *"Lord, help me!"*

Prayer doesn't get much simpler than that, does it? How many times have we found ourselves in dire straits, unable to think of anything to say except, "Lord, help me"? It is the most basic prayer known to humanity, and it is buried in the heart of every individual who has ever lived, including the most adamant atheist. It is an acknowledgment of our utter helplessness apart from God, a position from which miracles are born and lives transformed.

This particular situation with the Syro-Phoenician woman was exactly that. This mother was desperate. She had undoubtedly cared for her child for years, possibly even taking her to every charlatan that promised a cure in exchange for whatever meager pittance of coins she might possess. Yet the girl had not been healed. In fact, the mother described her daughter as being "*severely* demon-possessed." Her child was out of control, possibly even suicidal or dangerous to others. If anyone needed help, this poor woman qualified.

"*Lord, help me,*" she prayed, a shorter version of her first request when she referred to Jesus as the "*Son of David.*" No doubt she made this wise change of address when she realized the disciples' animosity toward her. The Jewish followers of Jesus did not want a Gentile woman hanging around, crying out and drawing attention to herself. When she understood perhaps that she had made a mistake by addressing Jesus as the Son of David, since she herself was not a daughter of Israel and therefore had no right to approach Him as a Jew of equal lineage, she changed her tactics. If she couldn't appeal to Him as a fellow Jew, she would throw herself on His mercy as Lord. She was, after all, a needy creature, and to acknowledge His ability to meet her need and to call Him Lord signified her recognition of Him, either as God Himself or at least as One who rightfully represented Him.

This was a huge step of faith for this formerly pagan woman, but when we are desperate to see the life of a loved one changed, we are more willing to take those steps of faith. But even then Jesus didn't immediately respond to her plea.

Instead, He said to her, "*It is not good to take the children's bread and throw it to the little dogs*" (Matthew 15:26). Ouch! That had to hurt. It was bad enough that Jesus ignored her the first time she cried out to Him, but now it seems as if He is purposely insulting her. How does that square with our picture of a loving Savior?

There are two Greek words for dog, and the distinction between the two is important. David H. Stern, in the *Jewish New Testament Commentary*, explains it this way:

> *There are two Greek words for "dog": "kuon," scavenging hounds that roam the street in packs, and "kunarion," small dogs kept as house pets (only in this passage and its parallel, Mk. 7:27-28). Yet even if Gentiles are not here compared with wild snarling beasts, are they still not being insulted? The answer can only be: no more than in the Tanakh [Old Testament] itself, where the people of Israel are taken by God in a special way as his children. And although Judaism teaches that the righteous Gentiles of the world have a share in the world to come, this is not a primary focus either in the Tanakh or in rabbinic Judaism.*

The amazing thing in this story is that the Syro-Phoenician woman does not take offense at all to this statement by Jesus. Instead, she perseveres in her humble way and says, *"Yes, Lord, yet even the little dogs eat the crumbs which fall from their masters' table"* (Matthew 15:27).

*One word from His mouth is enough to meet the need.*

Rather than be insulted or argue that she has a right to ask for healing for her daughter, this dear mother simply admits that what Jesus has said is absolutely and unquestionably true. Then she implies that to scavenge the crumbs that fall from the banquet table won't deprive the Jews of their rightful inheritance. In one simple statement, she has acknowledged the truth of Jesus's words and the right to the Jewish people to have first place in His ministry and teachings. She also places herself humbly at His feet and asks for crumbs, acknowledging that the slightest bit of His miraculous power or one word from His mouth is enough to meet the need she has so openly brought before Him.

It is the exact position needed to evoke a healing response from Jesus. This nameless, pagan, Gentile woman was about to receive the miracle she needed for her daughter.

## A FAITHFUL BELIEVER

How well I relate to this desperate mother! My youngest son, who was raised in church and knew the Truth, chose for a time to walk away from that truth and live in a way that brought unimaginable pain and fear to my heart. Oh, how I agonized and prayed for his return! Like the father of the prodigal son in Luke 15:11–32, I stood at the edge of the roadway, gazing longingly at the spot where my beloved son had turned away from his heavenly Father and started his trek into the far country. The hope of seeing him return kept me going through those long, painful months and years.

But this poor Syro-Phoenician woman hadn't had that hope, for she did not know nor did she follow the one true God. She no doubt prayed and offered sacrifices to every pagan god she ever heard about, but it wasn't until she heard stories of the One who walked the dusty roads of Galilee, forgiving sins and healing the sick and wounded, that a flicker of true hope began to burn in her heart.

Could it be? Was it possible that this One, whom some said was Israel's long-awaited Messiah, could in truth perform miracles? And if so, did this pagan, Gentile woman dare to hope that He would stoop to include her among the recipients of those miracles?

She knew her chances were slim, but even a slim chance is better than none when she'd already lived without hope for years. This mother had no doubt devoted the majority of her life to caring for this severely demon-possessed daughter whom, despite the problems her situation presented, she loved dearly. She was willing to humble herself, to beg, to throw herself on the mercy of the One who might be able—and willing—to help her.

Again, we have to remember that this was a woman with no

ancestral, national, or religious right to approach Jesus—or any other Jew, for that matter—to ask for a favor. Yet she did. Not only did she approach Him and ask for His help, she continued asking, even when it seemed He had rebuffed and insulted her. No wonder Jesus finally responded to her as He did, culminating in one of the most touching miracle stories in all of the Gospels.

With this humble woman admitting her willingness—even her eagerness—to accept whatever crumbs fell from the table at which only the Jewish people were entitled to sit, here is what happened: *"Then Jesus answered and said to her, 'O woman, great is your faith! Let it be to you as you desire.' And her daughter was healed from that very hour"* (Matthew 15:28).

*I have been that mother, desperately seeking help for a child.*

*"O woman, great is your faith!"* What a declaration from the very mouth of God incarnate! Isn't that a statement we too would like to hear directed toward us? I, on the other hand, am more inclined to expect to hear Jesus say to me as He did to the disciples in Matthew 6:30, *"O you of little faith."* Perhaps that's because my prayers aren't as desperate and humble as the prayers of this Syro-Phoenician woman for her daughter. Perhaps, when I still have a glimmer of hope that I can work things out on my own, I don't feel the total desperation and dependence on Him as did the mother whose child was "severely demon-possessed."

How is it that I so quickly and frequently forget what it's like to pray with such desperation? Is it because my once-prodigal son has come home from the pigpen and is now living a more respectable life? Does it take another such crisis to drive me to my knees and to cry out for even the crumbs that fall from the table of those more worthy than I?

This mother, whose deep love for her child drove her past her feelings of unworthiness to humble herself and persist in prayer to the only One who could help her, is a woman I relate to quite easily. I have been that mother, desperately seeking help for a child; I have been that woman, cloaked in unworthiness with no right to ask for the help I so desperately needed.

And so have we all. It is a place of humility and selflessness, the place where God can break through the facades and the masks that we all wear and meet the needs that cry out from our deepest pain. It is the place where the Syro-Phoenician woman found healing for her daughter—and, no doubt, eventual salvation for herself and others, for there is little doubt that this woman became a follower of the Jewish Messiah to whom she had come with such fear and trembling... and hope.

*"O woman, great is your faith!"* What a powerful proclamation, and one immediately followed by words that must have caused an explosion of joy in this woman's heart: *"Let it be to you as you desire"* (Matthew 15:28). It was no secret what it was that the woman desired, as she openly and repeatedly asked for it: help and healing for her severely demon-possessed daughter. So when Jesus spoke those words, she immediately knew that her petitions had been answered.

Isn't that the message and the heart of Psalm 37:4–11, that beloved section of Scripture that promises great peace and blessing to those who patiently and completely put their trust in God?

> *Delight yourself also in the LORD, and He shall give you the desires of your heart. Commit your way to the LORD, trust also in Him, and He shall bring it to pass. He shall bring forth your righteousness as the light, and your justice as the noonday. Rest in the LORD, and wait patiently for Him; do not fret because of him who prospers in his way, because of the man who brings wicked schemes to pass. Cease from anger, and forsake wrath; do not fret— it only causes harm. For evildoers shall be cut off; but those who wait on the LORD, they shall inherit the earth. For yet a little while and the wicked shall be no more; indeed, you will look diligently for his place, but it shall be no more. But the meek shall inherit the earth, and shall delight themselves in the abundance of peace.*

This particular passage of Scripture does not make the false promise that those who follow Jesus will never experience sorrow or trials or problems; it does, however, promise that those who submit their lives to His Lordship will ultimately rest in God's blessing and reward. In contrast, it also promises that those who refuse to repent and accept or follow the teachings of the Bible but instead continue on in their own way will one day be "cut off." When the desire of our heart is to lay everything at the feet of Jesus, submitting our very lives to His will and purpose, we shall have the desires of our heart and will delight ourselves *"in the abundance of peace."*

Part of the abundance of peace is a joy beyond imagining, and that's what that dear mother felt the day she heard Jesus say to her, *"O woman, great is your faith! Let it be to you as you desire."* Her desire was to see her daughter healed and delivered from severe demon possession, and verse 28 goes on to tell us *"And her daughter was healed from that very hour."* This mother's humble and persistent petitions were answered, and her daughter was healed.

One interesting thing to note here is that Jesus didn't have to leave where He was and go with the Syro-Phoenician woman to her home to lay hands on the daughter and cast out the demons by speaking to them. He simply made a statement of deliverance, and the woman believed Him. The daughter, who wasn't even in the immediate vicinity, reaped the benefits. By the time the mother returned home, no doubt running all the way and rejoicing as she went, her daughter was able to welcome her with open arms and a grateful heart.

When my prodigal was away from home, it gave me great comfort to know that despite the fact that he was out of my sight and my parental "jurisdiction," he was not out of God's. The "hound of heaven," as God's Spirit has often been called, was right on my son's heels. My part was simply to yield my will and submit my son to God—and to pray. The faithful Savior, who had once wooed and won my rebellious heart, would do the same for my son.

Did God tell me my faith was great during those days? Occasionally. More often, however, I was hanging on by my fingernails, wondering if I would make it through yet another difficult day, another tear-filled night. But always God was faithful—even when I wasn't. When I despaired of ever seeing my son repent and begin the long trek home from the pigpen, the everlasting arms were there to carry me through when I was too weak to continue putting one foot in front of the other. And that same faithful God, who carried me and pursued my son, who at last answered the Syro-Phoenician woman and healed her daughter, continues to carry and pursue, listen and answer, save and deliver today.

Though many have said that God does not answer the prayers of the unsaved, the story of the Syro-Phoenician woman and her severely demon-possessed daughter gives us pause to consider how God draws the unsaved to Himself. True, it was a desperate need that drove the woman to Jesus, but isn't that often the case for many of us? Few of us leave our lives of ease and self-sufficiency to seek a Savior when we don't believe we need one. But throw some desperate and very personal needs into the mix, and suddenly things change. When this formerly pagan mother placed her faith in Jesus, He honored that faith—even publicly commended her for it—and gave her the desire of her heart. As a result, it is highly probable that she became one of the first Gentile "followers of the Way," spreading the word about the Jewish Messiah in her hometown and, in effect, helping to pave the way for the Christian community that eventually was established in Tyre.

*I was hanging on by my fingernails.*

Thirty years after the meeting between Jesus and this Syro-Phoenician woman, the Apostle Paul had occasion to spend a week in Tyre. Referring to this visit, Acts 21:5 declares,

> *When we had come to the end of those days, we departed and went on our way; and they all accompanied us, with wives and children, till we were out of the city. And we knelt down on the shore and prayed.*

Who were these people who accompanied Paul and his companions, who prayed with them before sending them on their way? They were the people of Tyre, believers in Jesus and followers of the Way, as they were often called in those days—Christian Gentiles, some of whom may very well have known and been influenced by the woman whose daughter had once been severely demon-possessed but had been healed and delivered by the Jewish Messiah.

*In our own righteousness we can ask or expect nothing from God.*

James 4:2 says, *"Yet you do not have because you do not ask."* How many times do we fail to take a need to God in prayer because it just seems so overwhelming—or perhaps because we feel unworthy to ask? Of course we're unworthy! In our own righteousness we can ask or expect nothing from God. But that's why Jesus told us to ask in His name—because He is worthy and righteous, and He has extended that same worth and righteousness to those who receive Him as Savior and Lord. Therefore we never have to worry that we are not worthy to come into His presence. In fact, God longs for us to do so! Jesus extended that very invitation when He said,

*"Come to Me, all you who labor and are heavy laden, and I will give you rest. Take My yoke upon you and learn from Me, for I am gentle and lowly in heart, and you will find rest for your souls. For My yoke is easy and My burden is light."*
—Matthew 11:28–30

God wants us to come to Him—humbly, desperately, totally dependent on Him for everything, understanding that, as Jesus said, *"without Me you can do nothing"* (John 15:5). That's the place this pagan woman had found herself, and so she came, knowing there was no other hope for her, no other chance for her daughter. And Jesus, pleased by her faith, gave her the desire of her heart.

Getting past the sense of unworthiness that holds us back from asking for God's help is a very real challenge, but once we've done that, the next step is to understand that there is nothing too hard for God. As Jesus told His disciples when they asked how anyone could possibly be saved, *"With men this is impossible, but with God all things are possible"* (Matthew 19:26). God can do anything. Our worst circumstances are not a problem for Him.

Beyond the fact that God is *"able to do exceedingly abundantly above all that we ask or think, according to the power that works in us"* (Ephesians 3:20), meaning His ability to *do* goes far beyond our ability to *ask*, is the amazing fact that He loves us and wants to care for us and meet our needs, even though we may not always understand what those needs truly are. And unlike the poor Syro-Phoenician woman, we have been invited into His presence, invited to lay our petitions at His feet, invited to ask, seek, and knock. And when we answer His invitation, we hear Him say, as He did to this Canaanite woman, *"O woman, great is your faith! Let it be to you as you desire"* (Matthew 15:28).

*"What's the difference between a soccer mom and a pit bull? Lipstick."*
**—Sarah Palin, 2008 VP Candidate, Alaska Governor**

## Something to Think About/ Enter in Your Journal:

1. List some of the times you've felt a bit like the disenfranchised Syro-Phoenician woman with the severely demon-possessed daughter—unqualified, unworthy, unlovable, and in way over your head. As a result, you refrained from asking God for the help you truly needed.

2. What about the times when desperation finally drove you past those feelings of being unqualified, unworthy, and unlovable? Consider the difference that desperation made in the way you dealt with the problems, and then describe the outcome when you broke through and, with nowhere else to turn, laid your heart's desires at God's feet, desperate for the answer that only He could give.

3. Has anyone ever commended you on being a woman of great faith? How did you feel when you heard those words? Were you stunned, pleased, embarrassed? What did you say in response? Why do you suppose that person said such a thing to you in the first place? Finally, how did it change the way you viewed yourself from that point on?

*"No gift to your mother can ever equal her gift to you—life."*
**—Anonymous**

## A Mother's Prayer:

*Father God, I thank You that because of the life, death, and resurrection of Your Son, Jesus Christ, I don't have to cower in fear or hide in shame because I am unworthy to come into Your presence. You, Lord, have made a way, and You have invited me to come. Teach me, Lord, to do so—quickly and often, without waiting until I am in such dire and desperate straits that I am nearly destroyed. Teach me to come simply because it is the place I want to be—in Your presence, enjoying You as my heavenly Father, and knowing that Your love for me is greater than anything I can ever imagine. As a result, I can trust You to always do what's right and best for me—in Your time and in Your way, and most importantly, for Your glory. In Jesus's name I pray. Amen.*

**"Children are the anchors that hold a mother to life."**
**—Sophocles**

*"A mother's children are portraits of herself."*

—Author unknown

# CHAPTER 12

# Salome: Catching the Eternal Vision

*Then the mother of Zebedee's sons came to Him with her sons kneeling down and asking something from Him And He said to her, "What do you wish?" She said to Him, "Grant that these two sons of mine may sit, one on Your right hand and the other on the left, in Your kingdom."*
—Matthew 20:20–21

SUGGESTED SCRIPTURE READINGS:
Matthew 4:21; 20:20–28; 27:56; Mark 1:19–20; 10:35–40; 15:40–41; 16:1–8; John 19:25

Salome, whose name means "peaceable," is best known for the request she presented to Jesus regarding her two sons, James and John. But there is so much more about this faithful follower of the Savior than initially meets the eye.

Referred to most often in the Scriptures as the mother of James and John and the wife of Zebedee, a well-to-do fisherman, Salome was one of those who faithfully followed Jesus and supported His public ministry from beginning to end, and who no doubt knew Him even before that.

Zebedee and Salome, along with their two sons, more than likely lived in Capernaum, or possibly nearby Bethsaida, on the shores of the Sea of Galilee. The first chapter of Mark reveals that Zebedee had hired servants (see Mark 1:20), so we can assume that he was successful in his fishing business, and that the family was known and respected in the community. We can also assume that Salome had her hands full with her two lively sons, since they were referred to in Mark 3:17 as "Sons of Thunder," possibly due to their explosive natures.

Already, as mothers, whether or not we have sons, we can relate, can't we?

❖ ❖ ❖

Although it's possible that Salome had other children, they aren't mentioned in the Scriptures. Perhaps she had more sons, and even some daughters, but only James and John, the "Sons of Thunder," are mentioned and discussed in the Bible. Given that other children were not mentioned and that we learn from the Scriptures that Salome physically followed after and served Jesus during His public ministry, it's likely that she did not have younger children at home. Regardless, we will focus on Salome only as the wife of Zebedee and the mother of James and John—and, of course, as the faithful follower of the Jewish Messiah. For, ultimately, that is how she is defined throughout the Gospel accounts of her life—and how we best need to understand her if we are to emulate her as a mother and a disciple.

Immediately after the baptism of Jesus by His cousin John the Baptist, which formally initiated Jesus's approximately three years of public ministry, He spent some time in Capernaum, most probably the hometown of James and John, as well as another well-known fisherman named Simon Peter. It was during that early season of Jesus's public ministry, while He was in Capernaum, that He called these three to follow Him and become His disciples, so it is certainly not a stretch to imagine that Jesus spent time in the homes of these men and became acquainted with their families.

Perhaps Jesus enjoyed visiting James and John and eating Salome's cooking. Another possibility is that this relationship may have predated Jesus's public baptism. Some scholars believe

*Women not only followed, but also contributed to His financial support.*

that Mary, the mother of Jesus, and Salome, were sisters, based on the statement made in John 19:25: *"Now there stood by the cross of Jesus His mother, and **His mother's sister**, Mary the wife of Clopas, and Mary Magdalene"* (emphasis added). Whether or not that is the correct interpretation of that portion of John 19:25, it is certainly safe to conclude that, apart from Mary of Nazareth, Salome was one of the most notable mothers to cross Jesus's path during the three years of His public ministry, and their relationship was a close and trusted one. The very fact that Salome felt comfortable making what, to some, seemed a bold or even brazen request regarding her sons (see Matthew 20:20–23) speaks highly of the level of relationship between the Lord Jesus and Salome. In addition, it is clearly stated in Luke 8:1–3 and in Mark 15:40–41 that Salome, along with a sizeable band of other women, not only followed Jesus but also contributed to His financial support throughout His public ministry.

Whatever the bounds and parameters between these two families in general, and between Jesus and Salome in particular, the two were certainly more than casual acquaintances and had spent enough time together to be considered friends, earning Salome an honored place among the followers of the Jewish Messiah.

## LATE IN JESUS'S PUBLIC MINISTRY

As the three years of Jesus's public ministry as an "itinerant preacher" progressed, Salome continued to follow after Him. In addition to "ministering" to Jesus (see Mark 15:40–41), whether providing food or clothing or funds, or possibly friendship and prayer support, Salome must have listened to Him as He taught the multitudes. She no doubt marveled at the lessons He illustrated through His many parables, and was amazed at the miracles He performed by a touch or a word. This mother of two of Jesus's most trusted "inner circle" of disciples—the third being Peter—was certainly privy to inside information that might not be available to everyone who came to hear and receive from this benevolent Prophet and learned Rabbi.

It is also logical to assume that this dear woman believed strongly enough in the ministry of Jesus that she gave up a relatively comfortable lifestyle to follow Him in His ministry to the masses. Having come from a comfortable home where her fisherman husband, Zebedee, provided well for her, it must have been quite an adjustment to leave her home and live on the road.

Of course, she no doubt had the added incentive to remain close to her sons, particularly if James and John truly were her only children. We mothers tend to have a difficult time cutting those apron strings at times, and those very ties may have been at least part of the motivation that moved our heroine to begin a nomadic lifestyle. In fact, the story for which she is best known lends credence to that very supposition, and it is found in Matthew 20:20–28:

> Then the mother of Zebedee's sons came to Him with her sons, kneeling down and asking something from Him. And He said to her, "What do you wish?" She said to Him, "Grant that these two sons of mine may sit, one on Your

*right hand and the other on the left, in Your kingdom." But Jesus answered and said, "You do not know what you ask. Are you able to drink the cup that I am about to drink, and be baptized with the baptism that I am baptized with?" They said to Him, "We are able." So He said to them, "You will indeed drink My cup, and be baptized with the baptism that I am baptized with; but to sit on My right hand and on My left is not Mine to give, but it is for those for whom it is prepared by My Father." And when the ten heard it, they were greatly displeased with the two brothers. But Jesus called them to Himself and said, "You know that the rulers of the Gentiles lord it over them, and those who are great exercise authority over them. Yet it shall not be so among you; but whoever desires to become great among you, let him be your servant. And whoever desires to be first among you, let him be your slave— just as the Son of Man did not come to be served, but to serve, and to give His life a ransom for many."*

Interestingly, Mark tells the same story in such a way as to show that it was actually James and John who directly—rather than indirectly, through their mother—asked this question of Jesus:

*Then James and John, the sons of Zebedee, came to Him, saying, "Teacher, we want You to do for us whatever we ask." And He said to them, "What do you want Me to do for you?" They said to Him "Grant us that we may sit, one on Your right hand and the other on Your left, in Your glory." But Jesus said to them, "You do not know what you ask. Can you drink the cup that I drink, and be baptized with the baptism that I am baptized with?" They said to Him, "We are able." So Jesus said to them, "You will indeed drink the cup that I drink, and with the baptism I am baptized with you will be baptized; but to sit on My right hand and on My left is not Mine to give, but it is for those for whom it is prepared." And when the ten heard it, they began to be greatly displeased with James and John. But*

*Jesus called them to Himself and said to them, "You know that those who are considered rulers over the Gentiles lord it over them, and their great ones exercise authority over them. Yet it shall not be so among you; but whoever desires to become great among you shall be your servant. And whoever of you desires to be first shall be slave of all. For even the Son of Man did not come to be served, but to serve, and to give His life a ransom for many."*
—Mark 10:35–45

For the most part, these two versions of the same story are nearly identical, except that Matthew's has Salome asking Jesus for this great favor, while Mark's shows the "Sons of Thunder" as the ones who are "shooting off their mouths" and requesting special treatment. More than likely, since James and John and Salome all traveled with Jesus, all three of them approached Him to request this enormous favor. Who instigated it? The Scriptures don't explicitly answer that question. But we do know that when Jesus answered the three, He directed His words to James and John, not to Salome.

Perhaps this was because Jesus knew well what we can only guess at: that James and John put Salome up to approaching Jesus for them. Mothers are often and easily persuaded to "do the dirty work" for their children, covering for them and taking chances for them, but the Lord Jesus isn't fooled. Even if this were not the case and Salome had originally come up with the idea, it is still obvious from Jesus's answer that He knew the ambitious hearts of His disciples—and not just James and John.

First, Jesus responds to this request by speaking directly to the two about whom the request was made—the "Sons of Thunder" themselves. "You don't know what You're asking," He tells them, wanting them to understand that His kingdom is not of this world. They were hoping to follow Jesus into greatness and power on this earth, but Jesus was trying to get through to them that His greatness and power would never be found in material possessions or temporal rulership.

Jesus didn't stop there, of course, as this is a message He wants to convey to all who would follow Him—in those days, yes,

*It is still obvious from Jesus's answer that He knew the ambitious hearts of His disciples.*

as well as down through the ages since. So He turned to the rest of His disciples, who had already begun grumbling and showing their own pettiness and selfish ambitions by complaining about the audacity of James and John to make such a request. No doubt the other disciples had their own aspirations to greatness, and they didn't like being usurped by these two fishermen who just happened to have a good Jewish mama running interference for them.

*"You know that the rulers of the Gentiles lord it over them, and those who are great exercise authority over them,"* Jesus told the disciples after He *"called them to Himself"* (Matthew 20:25). *"Yet it shall not be so among you"* (Matthew 20:26).

Always that was the message Jesus tried to hammer home with His followers: *It's not about you; it's about serving God and others, for My kingdom is not of this world.* Every story Jesus told, every miracle He performed, every sermon He preached, every example He set was calculated to illustrate and enhance that great truth, a truth that runs completely opposite to the message and practice of this world. Those who belong to this world, who serve "the god of this world" (Satan) spend their entire lives seeking to serve themselves, to gain more money and material goods, more temporal pleasure and power and prestige. But Jesus wanted to make it clear that those who chose to follow Him would not live that way. *"Yet it shall not be so among you,"* He said in verse 26, and then went on to explain how it should be for those who claim to follow and serve Him.

> *"Whoever desires to become great among you, let him be your servant. And whoever desires to be first among you, let him be your slave—just as the Son of Man did not come to be served, but to serve, and to give His life a ransom for many."*
> —Matthew 20:26–28

Those who foolishly and selfishly limit their lives to this temporal world are out to serve and exalt number one, but Jesus said those who truly wish to be great should devote their lives to serving others, as He Himself had come to do. He even spoke to them prophetically of the great sacrifice He would soon make on the Cross to redeem sinners and open the door for relationship to be restored with God.

And that, of course, was the key element and point of this great story. It wasn't so much whether it was Salome or her sons who asked this monumental favor of Jesus—a favor that Jesus explained could only be granted by the Father—but that none of Jesus's followers should seek such prestige or position, but rather seek to have a servant's heart, even as their Master did.

*Somewhere during her ministry to Jesus, she caught the eternal vision.*

Finally, whether it was Salome's ambition for her sons that instigated this event or whether she simply went along with them in an effort to secure a positive response from Jesus, somewhere along the line, during her ministry to Jesus, she caught the eternal vision.

## AFTER JESUS'S DEATH

Not only was Salome present at least from the early days of Jesus's public ministry, if not before, but she was there to the very end—and beyond. When we next read of this dear woman, we find her standing at a distance, as Jesus hangs on the Cross, a thief on His right and another on His left. No doubt this woman, as well as the others with her, wept at the gruesome and nearly unimaginable sight of their beloved Teacher being crucified at the hands of the Roman soldiers, in complicity with some of the Jewish religious leaders. We know there were several women present because the Scriptures clearly state this fact:

> *There were also women looking on from afar, among whom were Mary Magdalene, Mary the mother of James*

*the Less and of Joses, and Salome, who also followed Him
and ministered to Him when He was in Galilee; and many
other women who came up with Him to Jerusalem.*
—Mark 15:40–41

Faithful Salome, who may very well have cooked meals for Jesus
when He first began His public ministry and chose her sons as
followers; who traveled with Him on the dusty roads of the Holy
Land, giving up her comfortable home and sleeping out in the
open under the stars; who listened and learned from His words
and His actions, may very well have realized that the fate that now
befell her Master could as easily befall her sons.

None of that was as she'd planned it, certainly not when she
and her "Sons of Thunder" approached Jesus, asking for a special
place in His kingdom. Standing there in the unnatural darkness
of that dreadful day, it must have seemed that all hope of a new
kingdom under the rule of Jesus of Nazareth had evaporated
before her eyes. What would she do now? Would she give up
and return to the life of a wife and mother of fishermen? Could
her sons indeed return to such a profession when Jesus Himself
had told them they would be "fishers of men"? How could such a
statement hold any truth or hope in light of this most recent and
tragic development? Jesus, the One who had been hailed as King
as He made His triumphal entrance into Jerusalem on the foal of a
donkey just a week earlier, now hung in agony, dying a criminal's
death.

As this mother stood, watching and waiting, where were her
sons? James, the older of the two, had joined the other disciples
and run away. But at least John, her baby, was still there, waiting
with Salome and the other women, including Jesus's mother,
weeping as they watched their beloved's last moments on earth
draw to a close.

Though Salome was a faithful follower of Jesus, with Him to
the end, she was not evidently the leader of the little band of women
who had traveled and ministered to Him. That position fell to Mary
Magdalene, and yet Salome was loved and trusted by all who were
closest to the Master. It was, in fact, her younger son, John, to

whom Jesus entrusted the care of His own mother, when from the Cross He said to John in John 19:27, *"Behold your mother!"* That same verse goes on to tell us, *"And from that hour that disciple [John] took her [Mary of Nazareth] to his own home."*

When Jesus breathed His last, even that was not the end of Salome's service and faithfulness to Him. Mark 16:1 tells us this about her service to Jesus after His death and burial: *"Now when the Sabbath was past, Mary Magdalene, Mary the mother of James, and Salome bought spices, that they might come and anoint Him."* Jesus's body had been placed in a tomb and left there throughout the Sabbath, but now that the Sabbath was over, these devoted women came to anoint His body for a proper burial. Little did they expect to find an empty tomb! Their primary concern at that point was how they would roll away the large stone that sealed Jesus's tomb.

> *Now that the Sabbath was over, these devoted women came to anoint His body.*

> *Very early in the morning, on the first day of the week, they came to the tomb when the sun had risen. And they said among themselves, "Who will roll away the stone from the door of the tomb for us?" But when they looked up, they saw that the stone had been rolled away—for it was very large.*
> —Mark 16:2–4

The problem of the stone had been solved, for it had been rolled away and the tomb was open. They did the next natural thing— they went inside the tomb to complete their mission, their final act of service to their Master. As the story goes on to explain, these women were in for quite a surprise.

> *And entering the tomb, they saw a young man clothed in a long white robe sitting on the right side; and they were alarmed. But he said to them, "Do not be alarmed. You seek Jesus of Nazareth, who was crucified. He is risen! He*

*is not here. See the place where they laid Him. But go and tell His disciples—and Peter—that He is going before you into Galilee; there you will see Him, as He said to you."*
—Mark 16:5–7

Not only was the stone rolled away and the tomb open, but there was an unusual being inside—someone very much alive! This someone was *"a young man clothed in a long white robe,"* and the sight of him alarmed the women, as it would any of us. As if that weren't enough, this man then told them, *"You seek Jesus of Nazareth, who was crucified. He is risen! He is not here."* This man, quite obviously an angelic messenger, did not deny that Jesus was indeed crucified, but he also gave them the best news ever heard on this planet—He is risen! He is not here. Now go and tell His disciples and followers what you have seen and heard. Begin to spread the news that will change the world—one soul at a time!

Dear Salome, the one who had been known as the wife of Zebedee the fisherman and the mother of the "Sons of Thunder," James and John, was now privileged to become one of the first to proclaim the gospel, the good news that the One who died now lives again. What a joy must have flooded the souls of these astonished women! Yet, as amazing and nearly incredible as the news was, they didn't hesitate to run from the tomb, back into town, to proclaim it to the rest of Jesus's heartbroken followers. Though Mark's account says that the women *"said nothing to anyone, for they were afraid"* (Mark 16:8), we can assume that meant they said nothing to anyone outside the circle of Jesus's followers, as Matthew explains in His account of the same event.

*But the angel answered and said to the women, "Do not be afraid, for I know that you seek Jesus who was crucified. He is not here; for He is risen, as He said. Come, see the place where the Lord lay. And go quickly and tell His disciples that He is risen from the dead, and indeed He is going before you into Galilee; there you will see Him. Behold, I have told you." So they departed quickly from*

*the tomb with fear and great joy, and ran to bring His
disciples word.*
—Matthew 28:5–8

Certainly the women were afraid. Who wouldn't be after such an
experience? But in obedience they went from the tomb and were
on their way to tell the disciples when something else happened,
as explained by Matthew.

*And as they went to tell His disciples, behold, Jesus met
them, saying, "Rejoice!" So they came and held Him by
the feet and worshiped Him. Then Jesus said to them, "Do
not be afraid. Go and tell My brethren to go to Galilee,
and there they will see Me."*
—Matthew 28:9–10

Now they had more than the empty tomb and the angel's word
to convince them of the Resurrection; they had the witness of the
resurrected Jesus Himself, who told them not to
be afraid but to go and tell Jesus's followers—
His "brethren," as He called them—to go to
Galilee where they too would see Him.

So the women followed the directions
of both the angel and their resurrected Lord,
and they told the good news to the disciples.
Salome, who had followed and ministered to
Jesus throughout His three years of public

*The women
followed the
directions of
both the angel
and their
resurrected Lord.*

ministry, was now privileged to be part of that band of women
who could tell firsthand of the amazing events that had taken
place on that great Resurrection Day. Though she had once gone
to Jesus—whether at her own volition or in response to her sons'
instigation—and sought special favor and position for those sons
in the earthly kingdom she erroneously imagined Jesus would one
day establish on earth, she now found herself in a humble but
honored position of declaring the true kingdom of the resurrected
Christ. What awe must have driven her, as well as the other women
with her, to proclaim this life-changing truth!

And what a joy must have followed in Salome's life from that day forward, as she saw her sons turned into bold witnesses for this eternal kingdom and its divine King, proclaiming the gospel and daily winning souls to Christ, until James was martyred for his faith and John banished to the Isle of Patmos where he wrote the great Book of the Revelation of Jesus Christ. What greater honor could any mother ever wish or pray for her child! Truly she and her sons had caught the eternal vision.

*"A wise woman once said to me: 'There are only two lasting bequests we can hope to give our children. One of these is roots; the other wings."*
**—Hodding Carter II, author and journalist**

SOMETHING TO THINK ABOUT/

## SOMETHING TO THINK ABOUT/ ENTER IN YOUR JOURNAL:

1. What are some of the dreams and ambitions you have hidden in your own heart regarding the future of your children? How can you know if those dreams and ambitions are God's purpose for your children—or your own?

2. Consider the times you have allowed yourself to "run interference" for your children when it might have been best to remain on the sidelines and pray. How did those situations turn out, and how might they have been different if you hadn't interfered?

3. How can you know if your personal dreams and ambitions for your children are one and the same as the eternal vision and purpose God has for them? If they are not the same, what "paradigm shift" would have to take place in your mother's heart for you to exchange those personal dreams and ambitions for the eternal vision God has purposed for them?

*"Men are what their mothers made them."*
**—Ralph Waldo Emerson, author, philosopher**

## A Mother's Prayer:

*Father God, I thank You that You know what's best for
my children, and others' children for whom I pray, and
You love them more than I ever could. I thank You too
that I can rest in the fact that Your plans for them are
for good and not for evil, to give them a future and
a hope (see Jeremiah 29:11). Give me a heart that is
willing to give up my personal dreams and ambitions for
my children, Lord, and exchange them for the greater
purposes and plans You have for them—whatever that
may involve. Help me to remember, Father, that they are
Your children, and that You have loaned them to me
for a short time, to love and to raise them for
Your honor and Your glory. I ask it, Lord,
in Jesus's wonderful name. Amen.*

**"Only God can give a mother the wisdom to be silent,
listen and not react when she really wants to shout
and scream!"**
**—Annetta Dellinger, author**

*"Christian motherhood far surpasses ties to the proverbial apron strings. It is a living link to the heart of God."*

—Charlotte Adelsperger and Karen Hayse, authors

CHAPTER 13

# Eunice and Lois: Passing the Torch

*To Timothy, a beloved son: Grace, mercy, and peace from God the Father and Christ Jesus our Lord. I thank God, whom I serve with a pure conscience, as my forefathers did, as without ceasing I remember you in my prayers night and day, greatly desiring to see you, being mindful of your tears, that I may be filled with joy, when I call to remembrance **the genuine faith that is in you, which dwelt first in your grandmother Lois and your mother Eunice**, and I am persuaded is in you also.*
—2 Timothy 1:2–5 (emphasis added)

SUGGESTED SCRIPTURE READINGS:
1 Samuel 1:28; Proverbs 4:11; 22:6; 23:25; 1 Timothy 6:20; 2 Timothy 1:2–7; 3:10–17

Though I wasn't raised in a Christian home, I came to know Jesus as my Savior when I was in my 20s and my children were still little. My youngest, in fact, was not born until the following year, so I quickly learned how important it was to instill in our children the faith that would sustain and guide them throughout their growing-up years and on into adulthood. However, I also had to learn that words are not enough. We can't simply tell our children—or anyone else, for that matter—about how much Jesus loves us and why it is so important to follow Him; we have to live our words in front of them daily. Not only has that been a difficult task, but I have learned it is an impossible one in my own strength. I could then, and can now, only model the Christian life as I learn to depend more and more on the Spirit of Christ living within me.

That, I am quite sure, is exactly why Lois and Eunice were able to set such a godly example for Timothy to follow, and why the Apostle Paul was able to express such confidence in the job these two women had done to successfully lead and guide Timothy to a strong walk as a believer.

❖ ❖ ❖

There is only one verse in the entire Bible that actually mentions Lois and Eunice by name; indirectly, there are many more that refer to them and/or exemplify their godly traits. Second Timothy 1:5 is the direct reference, written by the Apostle Paul to his beloved young protégé, Timothy: *"I call to remembrance the genuine faith that is in you, which dwelt first in your grandmother Lois and your mother Eunice, and I am persuaded is in you also."*

*Is there a mother or grandmother anywhere who could hope for more ?*

What a powerful statement! The apostle not only expressed his complete confidence in Timothy's Christianity, but he also declared his awareness that Timothy had come to that place of faith in Christ through the influence and teachings of his godly mother and grandmother. Is there a mother or grandmother anywhere who could hope for a more meaningful compliment or a more lasting legacy?

Timothy was born and raised in the city of Lystra in the Roman province of Galatia. Though his mother was a Jew, his father was Greek, and we have no record showing that Timothy's father ever came to faith in Jesus. However, it appears that either Timothy's father died when his son was very young, possibly even still an infant, or Timothy's parents had a loving and mutually respectful relationship, one in which Eunice was free to practice and pass on her Christian faith.

We also don't know from the Scriptures whether Lois came to faith first and then led her daughter to Christ, or whether both received Jesus as Savior at the same time. We do know that the word *grandmother* is used only once in the New Testament, and that is here in 2 Timothy 1:5, in reference to Lois. However conversion may have come to Lois and Eunice, it is obvious that theirs was a strong and devout faith, and that they actively lived it and passed it on through their words and actions to Timothy. Timothy, in turn, must have had a deep love and respect for both his mother and grandmother, and was eternally influenced because of them.

If it is true that Timothy's Greek father died while Timothy was still quite young, which many believe, then it is also quite probable that Eunice did what young widows without grown sons to care for them did in those days, and still do today: She went out and found some sort of job to support herself, her son, as well as her mother, Lois, who lived with them and undoubtedly cared for Timothy in Eunice's absence. Eunice may have labored in the fields, gleaning as Ruth did, or worked at some other profession, similar to New Testament businesswomen such as Priscilla or Lydia. Whatever the case, it is obvious that Grandmother Lois and Mother Eunice shared a deep love for one another and for little Timothy, doing whatever was necessary to see that his physical needs were met—and even more importantly, his spiritual needs.

For that truly is the meaning of Proverbs 22:6, which is so clearly epitomized by Lois's and Eunice's life: *"Train up a child in the way he should go, and when he is old he will not depart from it."*

How many times have we, as mothers or grandmothers, prayed and meditated upon that verse, claiming that great truth and promise for our own children or grandchildren, particularly when they stray from the faith? The key to seeing it lived out in our young ones' lives, however, is being sure that we have first lived it ourselves—both in word and deed.

How Lois and Eunice must have known and loved the Scriptures to be able to instill that same love in Timothy! And how they must have loved to gather together with other believers to hear those Scriptures preached and taught, to fellowship with others of like faith, and to encourage one another in that faith, particularly as persecution arose and intensified. There was no way these two women could have known what lay ahead for young Timothy, but they were obedient to God's Word to "train him up" in the love and admonition of the Scriptures, faithfully preparing him for whatever he might face in the days to come.

There is no greater pursuit or purpose to which we, as mothers, grandmothers, or community mothers can dedicate ourselves than properly training up those little ones who have been entrusted to us, teaching and modeling the only true faith and the way it should be lived on a daily basis. If we have done that, we can be sure that God will honor His word and faithfully draw our children and grandchildren into service for Him.

## PASSING THE TORCH

Regardless of how well we teach and model the Christian life to little ones, there comes a point in each of their lives when they must make that faith their own. For some that happens when they are still quite young; for others, the promise of Proverbs 22:6 doesn't come to fruition for many years—possibly even decades.

Such was the case for my beloved father, Hans. Born in Germany in 1911, he was only a young boy when his father went off to fight in the Kaiser's army. It wasn't long until the meager rations obtained in the seemingly never-ending soup lines and other deprivations of war took the life of Hans's younger brother and eventually landed Hans in a government-run hospital, where he was treated for scurvy. As he lay there in that hospital bed, miserable and brokenhearted, his little German mother, Jenny, sat at his bedside and sang hymns to him, songs that told of God's great love and faithfulness; of Jesus's death on the Cross, as well as His resurrection; and of heaven, where Hans would never be hungry or lonely again.

Finally, the war ended, Hans's father came home, and living conditions improved a bit. Two brothers and a sister were soon added to the family. When Hans, who was the oldest, turned 18, it was time for him to go out on his own and start a new life.

*With hopes and dreams of a better life to spur him on, Hans set sail for America.*

With hopes and dreams of a better life to spur him on, Hans set sail for America, where he had heard the streets were paved with gold and anyone could become rich if he was willing to work hard enough. Unfortunately, when Hans set foot in his new country, it was 1929, and the stock market crash destroyed his dreams of quickly amassing a fortune.

Seeing others standing in soup lines as he had done in Germany during World War I, Hans was determined to find a way to get through this economically difficult time without joining them. He found a job as a *vaquero* on a cattle ranch, and though the work was hard, the hours long, and the pay poor, he survived.

Then came World War II. As a US citizen, Hans joined the army and promptly found himself fighting against his homeland—including his two brothers who had been sucked into the Nazi war machine. But when the war finally came to an end, Hans and his family, with the exception of one brother, had all survived, and he immediately set about bringing them over to join him in America.

Once again he was united with his family, including his little German mother, Jenny, who had sung hymns to him and told him of God's great love throughout his boyhood years. Hans, however, had seen too much hardship and experienced too much pain to accept those teachings, and so he rejected them outright, proclaiming that he did not believe in God, and that even if God did exist, Hans wanted nothing to do with Him.

When Hans married and his wife and three children all came to the faith, Hans still refused to believe—until the last week of his 88 years on this earth. As his family despaired of ever reaching Hans with the loving message of the gospel, he began to experience a series of small strokes, each of which took him back a few more years to his former life. Within a matter of days, he had reverted to his childhood, speaking German and even singing some of the hymns his mother had taught him in his native tongue eight decades earlier.

As he lay on his deathbed, staring at something far away that his family could not see, the pastor who had come to visit and pray with him asked, "Hans, you know Jesus now, don't you?"

Though Hans couldn't respond verbally, his face lit up and he lifted his hand and pointed skyward, nodding his head in agreement and grinning from ear to ear. Days later, he smiled a final good-bye to his loved ones and silently slipped away to join his mother around the throne of the One she had taught him about so many years before.

What a merciful God we serve, that He would honor a mother's prayers and teachings, reaching out to an 88-year-old man on his deathbed and bringing him safely home. But how sad that Hans missed out on the joy of serving God throughout his lifetime.

Timothy was just the opposite. Trained up in the faith and watching his grandmother and mother model it—and no doubt being taken to worship services where he heard the Scriptures taught and fellowshipped with other believers—teenaged Timothy was "ripe" for conversion when the Apostle Paul travelled to Lystra in about A.D. 46. When Paul presented the gospel and the invitation to receive Jesus to Timothy, the teenager responded, giving over his heart and life to Christ.

Can't you just imagine the joy that exploded in the hearts of this faithful mother and grandmother? Their years of training and modeling a godly life had paid off. Timothy had taken on their faith as his own, making it personal and real, and assuring Lois and Eunice of the boy's salvation. Not only Proverbs 22:6, but others as well, must have echoed in their ears:

- *"I have taught you in the way of wisdom; I have led you in right paths"* (Proverbs 4:11).
- *"Let your father and your mother be glad, and let her who bore you rejoice"* (Proverbs 23:25).

This faithful and godly mother and grandmother had successfully passed the torch, and no they doubt heard the Lord whisper lovingly to them, "Well done, good and faithful servants."

## RELEASING TIMOTHY TO MINISTRY

Then, of course, came the hard part. Though their mother's and grandmother's hearts rejoiced in Timothy's salvation, they also had to accept that their season of teaching and training was over. It was time for Timothy to move on, time to take upon himself the cloak of ministry and to fulfill God's call on his life.

Is that ever an easy task for any woman who has loved and nurtured a child? Of course not. Though we want to see them grow up to be responsible adults who love and serve God with all their heart, we know that means they may very well leave us as they move out into that area of servanthood. And that hurts. But isn't that releasing of them to God's service exactly what Hannah meant when she declared in 1 Samuel 1:28, *"Therefore I also have lent him to the LORD; as long as he lives he shall be lent to the LORD"?*

*They may very well leave as they move out into servanthood... and that hurts.*

Let's face it, moms and grandmas, aunties and others. It's easier when they're home, safe under our watchful eye, and protected in our love and care. But inevitably time passes, and we suddenly have to release them to move on. Is it any wonder that our heart cries out in protest? However, if we have done our job, training our little ones up in the way they should go, we can trust that God, who loves them infinitely more than we, will carry them through all that He has purposed for them.

In Timothy's case, God brought the Apostle Paul into his life—and Timothy into Paul's—to fill a need in each of them. If we are right in assuming that Timothy's father had already died by this time, then Paul became the father figure that was missing in Timothy's life. Even if Timothy's father was living, he most likely was not a believer, as his conversion is never mentioned in the Scriptures, and therefore Paul still filled that needed role for Timothy.

Timothy, on the other hand, filled a need for Paul as well. The apostle never married or had children of his own, but we know that he became very attached to Timothy. In 2 Timothy 1:2–7, one of Paul's letters to Timothy, written while Paul was in prison because of his Christian witness, the apostle makes it quite clear what a close relationship the two had, and how Paul had come to think of young Timothy as his son in the faith:

> *To Timothy, a beloved son: Grace, mercy, and peace from God the Father and Christ Jesus our Lord. I thank God, whom I serve with a pure conscience, as my forefathers did, as without ceasing I remember you in my prayers night and day, greatly desiring to see you, being mindful of your tears, that I may be filled with joy, when I call to remembrance the genuine faith that is in you, which dwelt first in your grandmother Lois and your mother Eunice, and I am persuaded is in you also. Therefore I remind you to stir up the gift of God which is in you through the laying on of my hands. For God has not given us a spirit of fear, but of power and of love and of a sound mind.*

Not only had Paul come to consider Timothy his son, he had taken it upon himself to mentor and encourage the young man. It seems that Timothy may have been a bit fearful, which isn't too surprising when we consider the conditions under which they lived at that time. Christians were under severe persecution, often being tortured and even martyred for their faith. Timothy had begun his ministry at an early age, so he didn't yet have a lot of years of experience under his belt, and no doubt receiving encouraging words from his spiritual mentor and "adopted" father was quite helpful to him.

It is also evident that the Apostle Paul had great confidence in Timothy's faith, at least in part because he knew that the faith of Lois and Eunice, which had trained and nourished the young man from infancy, was strong and genuine. His closing admonition to Timothy in his first letter to him was worded as a reminder of those things he had been taught by his mother and grandmother, and a warning to avoid the false teachings of others:

> O Timothy! Guard what was committed to your trust, avoiding the profane and idle babblings and contradictions of what is falsely called knowledge—by professing it some have strayed concerning the faith. Grace be with you. Amen.
> —1 Timothy 6:20–21

Paul was reminding Timothy that if he stayed true to what he knew, to those teachings that had been instilled in him by his mother and grandmother all the years he was growing up, then he would not be deceived. He could trust the truth that was in him—God's truth, first imparted to him by Lois and Eunice—to keep him safe and on the right path. Paul knew that Lois and Eunice had trained Timothy up in the way he should go, and he therefore encouraged the young man not to stray from that truth.

It seems Paul had confidence that Timothy would heed his advice, as the young man had already shown himself to be faithful and true to the teachings of both his mother and grandmother, as well as of Paul.

> But you have carefully followed my doctrine, manner of life, purpose, faith, longsuffering, love, perseverance, persecutions, afflictions, which happened to me at Antioch, at Iconium, at Lystra—what persecutions I endured. And out of them all the Lord delivered me. Yes, and all who desire to live godly in Christ Jesus will suffer persecution.

*But evil men and impostors will grow worse and worse, deceiving and being deceived. But you must continue in the things which you have learned and been assured of, knowing from whom you have learned them, and that from childhood you have known the Holy Scriptures, which are able to make you wise for salvation through faith which is in Christ Jesus. All Scripture is given by inspiration of God, and is profitable for doctrine, for reproof, for correction, for instruction in righteousness, that the man of God may be complete, thoroughly equipped for every good work.*
—2 Timothy 3:10–17

Timothy had been learning from his mentor, Paul, and modeling his life accordingly. Paul wanted Timothy to understand that even as the young man had faithfully followed Paul in doctrine and teaching and lifestyle, so also he might have to follow him in sufferings and trials. "But don't worry," Paul told him. "Just as the Lord sustained me through everything I have had to endure, so He will do for you."

*He couldn't give false hope.*

Paul knew Timothy—and all believers—needed to hear this message of encouragement. As a faithful spiritual father and leader, he couldn't give false hope by saying that God would protect Timothy and never allow him to suffer, but he could assure him that the same God who loved him enough to die for him would also see him through any trials he might face in the future.

*"All who desire to live godly in Christ Jesus will suffer persecution,"* Paul told Timothy—and that promise has echoed down through the centuries, around the globe, in the ears of believers everywhere. Those who live in an environment where they are relatively free to practice and proclaim their faith may never have experienced the type of persecution that Christians in other places and times have been forced to endure. We can be grateful for that, of course, but it doesn't mean we don't suffer persecution or harassment for our faith in other ways. Whether

it's the abandonment of a loved one who doesn't share our beliefs, the loss of a job or promotion, or the taunts of the ungodly when we take a stand for righteousness, there is always a price to pay for being a Christian. Having the benefit of being trained when we were young in the way we should go will certainly help when such incidents occur and our depth of faith is tested.

What does Paul tell Timothy is the answer to standing strong when others try to pull us off-center from our faith? The Holy Scriptures, the Bible, the uncompromising Word of God, which Paul reminds Timothy that the young man has known since his childhood when his faithful mother and grandmother taught and modeled those Scriptures to him. *"All Scripture,"* Paul tells Timothy, *"is given by inspiration of God, and is profitable for doctrine, for reproof, for correction, for instruction in righteousness, that the man of God may be complete, thoroughly equipped for every good work"* (2 Timothy 3:16–17).

Paul wanted Timothy to understand that everything he would ever need in order to stand strong in the faith, to fulfill all that God had called him to do, was contained within the God-breathed words and instruction of the Scriptures. This is why Paul, in 2 Timothy 2:15, admonished Timothy to daily read and study and meditate on the Scriptures: *"Be diligent to present yourself approved to God, a worker who does not need to be ashamed, rightly dividing the word of truth."*

By staying faithful to the Word of God, which Timothy's grandmother and mother had taught him and which Paul had helped him understand even more clearly and now warned him to continue studying, the young minister of the gospel could remain true to his calling. Timothy could remain on the right path—the way which he had been trained up to follow from his earliest days by two women who were "good and faithful servants" and who loved Timothy enough to give him up to God's calling on his life.

## SOMETHING TO THINK ABOUT/
## ENTER IN YOUR JOURNAL:

1. Make a list of all those young lives you influence regularly: children, grandchildren, nieces, nephews, friends' and neighbors' children, children's classmates or fellow scouts, church friends. Ask yourself how you have taught and mentored them through your words and life example. How might you strengthen or improve your influence in their lives?

2. Consider times when some of these children have commented to you or others about your influence on their lives. Were you ever surprised by their comments, not having realized that you were indeed influencing them in one way or another? How did that make you feel? How do you think your influence might have an impact on their spiritual lives in the future?

3. Have you ever spiritually "adopted" a young person? If so, what were the positive (and possibly negative) effects of that relationship? If you are still in the relationship, how is it going? Do you see ways you might improve it? If the relationship has ended, do you have fond memories of the time you spent together? Are you pleased with the influence you had on that young person's life? Has he or she ever expressed to you what your investment of time and mentoring meant in his or her life? Have you ever released that young person you were mentoring to move on for some reason? How did you handle that?

*"Nurturing a good marriage goes a long way toward nurturing a child."*
**—Elaine W. Miller, author**

## A Mother's Prayer:

*Heavenly Father, thank You for the incredible opportunity and privilege You have given us to minister to and mentor young people, whether our own children and grandchildren, or someone else's. Thank You for the godly example You have given us in the Scriptures of Lois and Eunice, training up Timothy in the way he should go, and also of the Apostle Paul, who willingly stepped into Timothy's life to mentor and guide him. Help us, Lord, to follow in their footsteps and faithfully pour out our own lives to train and mentor those who need to know You and to fulfill Your purposes for their life. Father, please help us, too, when the time comes, to release them into Your service; to be willing to let go, even when it hurts and our hearts cry out in protest. Teach us to trust You, Lord, to carry them through whatever trials or sorrows they may face, knowing that You love them so much more than we ever could. We ask it, Lord, in Jesus's precious name. Amen.*

**"I love the women who raised Timothy, perhaps because Eunice and Lois remind me of Donna and Goldie, my mother and grandmother. My grandmother raised five daughters and one son on a widow's mite and then, when her baby girl, my mother, found herself divorced and a single mother, she took up her apron again."**
**—Marilynn Griffith, author**

"*My mother was the most beautiful woman I ever saw. All I am I owe to my mother. I attribute all my success in life to the moral, intellectual, and physical education I received from her.*"

—George Washington, US President

# CHAPTER 14

# The Proverbs 31 Woman: A Woman for All Seasons

*Her children rise up and call her blessed; her husband also, and he praises her: "Many daughters have done well, but you excel them all."*
—Proverbs 31:28–29

SUGGESTED SCRIPTURE READINGS:
Proverbs 31:1–31

One of the biggest problems we have as women when we read Proverbs 31 is the feeling that we can never measure up. This ideal and seemingly perfect woman is not only pure and godly, but she is also devoted to her family and community and to those who work for her, successful in her business ventures, and seemingly tireless in her efforts to serve everyone and everything around her. When we read her glowing description and then look in the mirror, the inevitable comparison can be more than slightly discouraging.

It doesn't have to be. When we take the time to carefully examine this remarkable woman's life and begin to understand who she really is—or, at least, who she represents—we can then begin to find great comfort in having her as our personal role model. With that in mind, let's look a little closer at this phenomenal Proverbs 31 woman of virtue.

❖ ❖ ❖

In addition to being called "the Proverbs 31 woman," this well-known person of the Old Testament Scriptures is also referred to as "the virtuous woman," a praiseworthy title indeed! The word *virtuous,* of course, denotes this special woman's piety and purity, and it is also the same word used to describe Ruth in Ruth 3:11, when Boaz, the man who would one day become her husband, says to her, *"And now, my daughter, do not fear. I will do for you all that you request, for all the people of my town know that you are a virtuous woman."*

This complimentary word denotes more than simply a high moral standard, however; it also attributes to both the Proverbs 31 woman and to Ruth the Moabitess the successful characteristic of having "proven abilities," As Sue and Larry Richards put it in *Women of the Bible, virtuous* carries overtones of valor, nobility, aristocracy. As we read through this familiar passage of Scripture, we will see that attribute of proven abilities mentioned many times over in the virtuous woman's life.

## THE UNNAMED WOMAN

The first few times I read through this particular chapter, I wondered why this amazing woman had remained anonymous. Wouldn't you think that anyone with that many positive attributes and accomplishments would have her name in print for all to see?

Then I thought again and realized that it may well have been because of those very qualities that not only did God choose to preserve her anonymity, but she may have chosen the same. Maintaining humility when your accomplishments are so numerous and everyone is extolling your praises would be difficult for anyone, even the Proverbs 31 woman. Remaining anonymous, therefore, helps preserve those humble qualities that so impress us as readers.

So who was this nameless woman of such great success and virtue? This chapter is the final one in the Book of Proverbs, and it is also found at the end of a chapter whose title and early verses mention King Lemuel and his mother, sparking the question as to the identity of this specific king. With no readily available or satisfactory answer to that question of King Lemuel's identity, we really can't draw any conclusions that would apply to the identity of the Proverbs 31 woman.

King Solomon is thought to have penned the Book of Proverbs, and if that is so, it is possible that this particular chapter may have been written about his mother, Bathsheba. Throughout the Book of Proverbs, and specifically in the early verses of Proverbs 31, we often come across references that read like a parent addressing and instructing a child. This particular chapter, in fact, begins in a style reminiscent of an instruction manual from a mother to a son, with the first nine verses telling the son how to live a godly life himself. Verses 10–31 then go on to tell him how to find a godly wife, which it implies is a good and wise thing to do, thus lending itself to the theory that Solomon wrote this particular proverb in honor of his mother who no doubt instructed him on like subjects, though sadly, as we see in his latter years, he didn't always heed her advice. However, most modern scholars don't accept the theory that Proverbs 31 was written by Solomon in honor of Bathsheba. So again, we are left to speculate and wonder as to the identity of the virtuous woman extolled in this proverb.

Perhaps the most likely explanation for the fact that such a prominent woman of the Old Testament is left unnamed is that she is simply too perfect to be any one particular individual, but rather is an ideal composite of the perfect wife, mother, and businesswoman. She certainly does embody most of the admirable traits of the other Old Testament women, and therefore typifies what we as modern-day women would also like to reflect in our own lives.

The Proverbs 31 woman has long been an admired source of inspiration for women throughout the centuries, in various cultures and walks of life, with her timeless and universal qualities that appeal to both men and women of all generations. Men especially find Proverbs 31 to be a helpful guide in finding their ideal mate, as outlined in the final 22 verses of this chapter. In fact, in the Hebrew language, each successive verse of these 22 verses begins with a letter that forms an acrostic, which has often been called "the ABC of the Perfect Wife," Deen says in her book. Again, this "perfect wife/mother" or "perfect woman" picture can be encouraging...or intimidating, depending on our understanding of who this Proverbs 31 woman is—and how she might, or might not, realistically relate to the rest of us "not-so-perfect" wives, mothers, and women.

*Her timeless and universal qualities appeal to both men and women of all generations.*

## THE "EVERYWOMAN"

One of the things that makes this Proverbs 31 woman so outstanding is her timeless and universal appeal. Despite the uncertain identity of this virtuous woman, it is believed by many that she is literature's most perfect picture of the ideal woman, and that this ideal woman most likely lived—or was portrayed to have lived—in the Eastern, Hebrew culture, more than 2,000 years ago. And yet, though we would expect to find a portrait of such a woman living in such a time and place to reflect one who was severely restricted by the male dominance of her time, we actually see that quite the opposite was true—at least, in her case. The words and attributes that best describe this woman include her generosity, efficiency, wisdom, sincerity, purity, godliness, and, of course, her love for her husband, her children, and others beyond her immediate family.

The final 22 verses of this final chapter in Proverbs open with both a question and a statement: *"Who can find a virtuous wife? For her worth is far above rubies"* (Proverbs 31:10). This question sets the tone for the following 21 verses, while the statement tells us that the writer of these verses—and, ultimately, God Himself, since He is the Author of the Scriptures from start to finish—has a high regard for a virtuous wife, declaring that her worth is *"far above rubies."* In essence, the writer is saying that a virtuous wife is priceless.

While the verses that follow this question and statement tend to describe a woman of relatively high social and economic status and, therefore, may not reflect the day-to-day existence or activities of the average woman of that culture and era, the general principles apply—not only to women of that particular time, but to women of all eras and cultures.

*The Proverbs 31 woman is, in essence, the Everywoman.*

The Proverbs 31 woman is, in essence, the Everywoman, the epitome of what every husband would love to have as a wife and every wife would like to be as a successful woman. The problem is that in studying an Everywoman model, it's easy to fall into the trap of thinking we can never measure up. But since each of us is only one woman and not many or all women, we will no doubt gain more from this study if we approach it from the angle that no one human being can contain or exhibit or achieve all of these many qualities and accomplishments. In that light, let's examine these verses regarding the virtuous woman's characteristics and see if we can better understand and put them into proper perspective so they won't seem quite so intimidating or overwhelming.

*Who can find a virtuous wife? For her worth is far above rubies. The heart of her husband safely trusts her; so he will have no lack of gain. She does him good and not evil all the days of her life.*
—Proverbs 31:10–12

These verses tell us that this Everywoman is not only virtuous and priceless, but she is also trustworthy and honorable, one who devotes her life to doing good, rather than evil. Goodness is her lifestyle, flowing from a good and pure heart.

The next seven verses point out the type of worker she is:

> *She seeks wool and flax, and willingly works with her hands. She is like the merchant ships, she brings her food from afar. She also rises while it is yet night, and provides food for her household, and a portion for her maidservants. She considers a field and buys it; from her profits she plants a vineyard. She girds herself with strength, and strengthens her arms. She perceives that her merchandise is good, and her lamp does not go out by night. She stretches out her hands to the distaff, and her hand holds the spindle.*
> —Proverbs 31:13–19

The Proverbs 31 woman is certainly no slouch! According to these verses, she actively seeks out the work that needs to be done, and then willingly throws herself into doing whatever is necessary to see it accomplished. If the provision her family needs isn't readily available, she goes wherever she must to obtain it, starting as early in the day as necessary to complete her tasks. Not only does she do this for her family, but for her maidservants as well. Most of us don't relate to having maidservants, but this principle of caring for others—whether employees or friends or neighbors—certainly applies at all levels.

This Everywoman also exercises wisdom in her investments, making wise business decisions and helping to bring in the necessary profit to sustain the household. She *"girds herself with strength,"* meaning she keeps herself in as good health and physical condition as possible so she can carry out her many duties. And though she is a woman of financial means with servants of her own, she actively works alongside her servants whenever necessary to see that the work is done correctly and on time, and that the goods that are produced are of top quality.

Quite obviously, in addition to being a faithful wife and mother, the virtuous woman of Proverbs 31 is also a wise and respectable businesswoman.

*She extends her hand to the poor, yes, she reaches out her hands to the needy. She is not afraid of snow for her household, for all her household is clothed with scarlet. She makes tapestry for herself; her clothing is fine linen and purple.*
—Proverbs 31: 20–22

These three verses show us that this woman, though fairly wealthy herself, has a deep concern for those who have less and that she uses her financial means to help them any way she can. Her heart for the poor is reflected in her actions and modeled to her family, particularly her children, so they might grow up to appreciate their financial and social position and develop loving and generous hearts as well. This wise and virtuous woman also makes certain that not only she but her entire household—family members and servants—are properly clothed, regardless of the weather.

*Her husband is known in the gates, when he sits among the elders of the land.*
—Proverbs 31:23

Here we see that even in such a male-dominated culture and time, not only is the Proverbs 31 woman known as her husband's wife, but he too is known and respected by the elders and other men in the community as the husband of this virtuous wife. The Proverbs 31 husband is able to hold his head high because he knows he has a godly wife at home, attending to those many functions required for running a successful household.

She makes linen garments and sells them,
and supplies sashes for the merchants.
*—Proverbs 31:24*

This verse tracks with verse 16, which says, *"She considers a field and buys it; from her profits she plants a vineyard."* If there was ever any doubt that this Proverbs 31 woman was a wise and successful businesswoman in her own right, these two verses dispel that doubt, confirming that she not only works hard to supply well-made goods, but that she turns a profit while doing so and then uses that profit to reinvest in other business ventures.

> *Strength and honor are her clothing; she shall rejoice in time to come. She opens her mouth with wisdom, and on her tongue is the law of kindness. She watches over the ways of her household, and does not eat the bread of idleness.*
> —Proverbs 31:25–27

These verses show clearly that a virtuous woman is to be honored, not only for the work she does but also for the wisdom she contributes to those who live in her household, whether husband, children, or servants. Sensitive to the things going on around her, this wise woman offers loving counsel to all who are willing to listen—and wise enough to apply her advice.

> *Her children rise up and call her blessed; her husband also, and he praises her: "Many daughters have done well, but you excel them all." Charm is deceitful and beauty is vain, but a woman who fears the LORD, she shall be praised. Give her of the fruit of her hands, and let her own works praise her in the gates.*
> —Proverbs 31:28–31

Ah, here we have it—the pièce de résistance, the Proverbs 31 woman's reward for being such a faithful and virtuous wife, mother, and businesswoman: her husband and children stand to their feet when she enters the room and proclaim that she is more blessed and valuable than any other woman they know. What do they give as their reason for such a proclamation? Truly it is because of the many attributes and accomplishments we have just discussed, but their specific reason is this: *"A woman who fears the LORD, she shall be praised."*

Why would her family make such a declaration? Proverbs 9:10 answers that question this way: *"The fear of the LORD is the beginning of wisdom, and the knowledge of the Holy One is understanding."* We saw in our verse-by-verse overview of this chapter of Proverbs that this virtuous woman exercised great wisdom and understanding in all areas of her life; her family recognized and honored that, stating that such wisdom and understanding could come only from one who fears—honors, loves, and respects—the Lord. Certainly this amazing Everywoman fits the bill to a T!

*Ah, here we have it— the pièce de résistance.*

## THE SEASONAL WOMAN

Understanding that this "perfect woman" is more of a composite of many women, rather than a portrait of one, makes looking in the mirror and searching for her reflection a lot less discouraging. And yet we can still find ourselves coming up as seriously deficient in the comparison game if we aren't careful to remember one very important point: Even the most devoted wife, woman, mother, and/or businesswoman can't do it all—and certainly not all at once! In fact, God never designed it to be so, and doesn't intend for us to try.

We all have seasons in our lives, and we may very well find ourselves in different seasons than those with whom we compare ourselves—and particularly so when that comparison is with the Proverbs 31 woman. Remember, this woman had financial means that many of us don't possess. She had servants, so she may not have had to make all the beds in the morning or fix breakfast for the kids before they left for school or water the plants or take out the trash or remember to toss something in the slow cooker before rushing off to work. And quite possibly, though she had children at home, they may very well have been beyond toddler or preschool age. If they weren't, they may have had a nanny to help care for them. If they were teenagers, even if they needed a lift to camel-riding practice or a shofar recital, the household help may have included a fulltime chauffeur for such time-consuming events.

Life is busy, and we all get caught up in it. Living in a "pull yourself up by the bootstraps," "I can do it myself," "more is better," "time is money" society, it's easy to become deceived into thinking we have to "do it all" and "be it all" all the time and at any cost, when in reality, a successful life is more about timely priorities and wise choices.

*A successful life is more about timely priorities and wise choices.*

Personally, I am in a season in my own life when I have a bit more freedom than I did when my children were little, and yet not as much freedom as I had a few years ago, after my children first left home to begin their own lives. You see, my mother, who is in her late 80s, now lives with us, and though her mind is sharp and clear, her body simply won't do many of the everyday tasks it once did quite easily. As a result, I choose to step in and do much of it for her. When the sheets on her bed need changing or her laundry needs washing, I put on my maid's cap. When she has a doctor's appointment, I switch to my chauffeur's hat. When she is hungry, I slip on my cook's apron. It's simply the season of life that I'm in right now.

Decades ago, however, I was in a very different season, one in which my mother did all those things for me, while I watched and learned about serving others. Just as they did in my life, seasons change, and with those changes come changes in responsibilities. This season I'm in right now will one day change as well, and I'll rejoice in knowing my dear mother is finally home with the Savior she has loved for so many years. Though I'll once again have more freedom to pursue other things, our home will be a quieter and lonelier place.

Somehow I can't help but believe that if I had a chance to ask this virtuous Proverbs 31 woman the question about how to handle the changing seasons of life with grace and wisdom—something she was quite obviously good at doing—she would answer something like this: "Slow down. Enjoy the season you're in, and stop trying to rush through it to the next one, for it will arrive soon enough. And once the next season is here, the former one is gone forever, becoming a memory that you don't want to regret because you didn't appreciate it when you had the chance."

A longtime friend of mine, whom I'll call Susie, had a young son named Jonathan. Jonathan was an adorable little boy, but quite rambunctious and active and loud as a little boy might be. When Susie got married at the age of 25 and became pregnant soon after, she and her husband, Tom, made the decision that she should leave her career, at least for a time, and devote herself fulltime to motherhood. Susie often told me that though she didn't regret that decision, there were times she desperately missed her work and looked forward to the day when she could return to it once again.

Then, one day, when Tom had taken Jonathan for a ride, a drunk driver plowed through a red light and smashed into the car in which Tom and Jonathan were riding. Though the drunk driver walked away without a scratch, Tom and Jonathan were killed instantly. In a moment's time, Susie not only lost her entire family, but that particular season of her life was ripped away forever, and she was thrown into a new season, one that seem characterized by storms and heartache.

*Appreciate whatever season you're in.*

Not long after that tragic event, Susie told me that she was back to working full time—and even overtime—in her career. Although it was going well, she admitted she would gladly give it up to be back in her previous season of life, staying home and caring for her precious husband and child.

"Don't wish your life away," she cautioned me. "Appreciate whatever season you're in, whatever God has given you to do. And do it with all your heart, for every day you are able. You never know when your season may change, and then you can never get it back."

Years ago there was a movie titled *A Man for All Seasons*. I don't remember anything about the movie itself, but I do know the premise of the title is faulty. No one man—or woman—can live in all seasons at once. But God can...and He does. Knowing that fact enables us to breathe a big sigh of relief, to stop living in regret, gazing in the mirror and seeing a big F for failure stamped on our forehead because we think we don't measure up to the virtuous Proverbs 31 Everywoman. It enables us to realize that all we have to do is be faithful today, in the season and circumstances of life where God has planted us. When we do that, we can be confident that others will rise up and call us blessed, and will say of us, *"Many daughters have done well, but you excel them all"* (Proverbs 31:29).

> *"Sometimes, I wonder what kind of legacy*
> *I'm leaving my children. Hopefully, my epitaph will*
> *read something like this: 'She hated folding laundry,*
> *but liked to fold us in her arms.'"*
> **—Dena Dyer, author**

## SOMETHING TO THINK ABOUT/ ENTER IN YOUR JOURNAL:

1. Have you ever found yourself getting caught up in the "comparison game," watching others and numbering their many attributes while despairing of ever being able to achieve them yourself? How did that make you feel? Knowing what you know now about the Proverbs 31 woman, what can you do to help prevent yourself from falling into that trap again?

2. Who are some of the women in your life who are or have been role models, and what is it about them that affects you so positively? Make a list of those attributes that drew you to them, and then ask yourself honestly which of those attributes you've been able to assimilate into your life. Which of those attributes have you not assimilated? Why do you think that is? Is there something you can do to remedy that, or is it possible that God has designed you differently and doesn't expect you to have some of the same characteristics as the women who have served as role models in your life?

3. Now consider those same women role models you've observed over the years, and make a list of their accomplishments. How do you feel when you read over that list? Is it encouraging and inspirational to see the things they've done and then aspire to do similar things? Or is it overwhelming because you feel you could never begin to accomplish anything even close to what they have done? How does it put this "ideal woman" image into better perspective if you break down these accomplishments into various seasons of life?

*"My mother, her four sisters, and my grandmother took me to church, forced me onto the stage to recite the verses that comfort me today, and most of all, they showed me what it means to be the hands and heart of Jesus to someone else."*
—**Marilynn Griffith, author**

## A Mother's Prayer:

*Father, help me to see this virtuous Proverbs 31 woman through Your eyes, from Your perspective and vantage point, from Your timeless view of the panorama of our lives. Help me to aspire to all You have purposed for me, but in Your time and for Your glory, and always with the clear remembrance that I can't achieve any of it in my own strength.*

*Lord, as I go about my days, living through the various seasons of life that You have prepared for me, help me to remember that others are looking at me, considering me a role model, aspiring to become like me. I am humbled at the thought, Father, and I want to be a worthy role model. Remind me daily, Lord, that I can fulfill that calling only as I trust in and rely on You each step of the way. I can never become that Proverbs 31 Everywoman, but I can become what You've called and gifted me to be as I learn to faithfully follow after You. In Jesus's name. Amen.*

**"I believed my children's outcome was totally dependent on me. Therefore, I alone had the total overwhelming responsibility for molding and shaping them. I was a whirling dervish, constantly at work, nonstop, going, going, going, doing, doing, doing. Now I'm more about being. Who am I being for my kids, not what am I doing for them."**
**—Laura Greiner, author**

*"The mother's heart is the child's schoolroom."*

—Henry Ward Beecher, clergyman, abolitionist

CHAPTER 15

# Mary: In a Class by Herself

*Then Mary said, "Behold the maidservant of the Lord!*
*Let it be to me according to your word."*
—Luke 1:38

SUGGESTED SCRIPTURE READINGS:
Matthew 1; 2; 12:46–50; 13:55; Mark 3:31–35; Luke
1; 2; 8:19–20; John 2:1–11; 7:5; 19:25–27; Acts 1:14

Though most mothers would think they could
never relate to this very special young virgin who
conceived a Child by the Holy Spirit and brought God's
redemption to earth in the form of His Son, Jesus, we
may have more in common with Mary than many would
imagine. God called Mary to set aside her own life to
bring forth His life, a life that would be given for the
forgiveness of sins for anyone who would repent and

turn to Him. God often calls us as mothers to lay aside our own dreams and desires in order to nurture young lives for God, lives that will go forth and help bring that message of the remission of sins to the inhabitants of a lost and dying world.

As Mary "pondered in her heart" the many things God spoke to her regarding her beloved Son, so we as mothers are called to do the same. And so, too, as Mary allowed Jesus to be conceived and grow within her until He was birthed into the world, we must allow God's Spirit to bear life in and through us as well. It is all about coming to that place of faith where we can say, regardless of the circumstances or their possible outcome, *"Let it be to me according to your word."*

❖ ❖ ❖

*In a class by herself.* Has there ever been a woman about whom those words more aptly applied? I don't believe so. Yet it wasn't Mary's beauty or her social status or even her virginity and purity that set her apart in that special class; it was the fact that the God of Israel—in His sovereignty—chose her to bring forth His Son into the earth—and her faith and submission to God that enabled it to be so.

Could Mary have chosen not to submit to God's plan for her life, to yield to fear and doubt instead of faith? Of course she could. God has given us all free will, and that means we can choose to submit God's plan for our lives—or not. If Mary had said no to God, He could certainly have used another virgin to bring forth His Son. Our disobedience or lack of faith does not thwart God's plans. However, God knew Mary's heart before He ever sent the angel Gabriel to speak to her, and so the outcome was assured. A study of the life and faith of this very special mother can help the rest of us find that place of assurance and fulfill God's purposes in our own lives, as well as in the lives of the children we influence.

*We can choose to submit to God's plan for our lives— or not.*

# A Nice Jewish Girl

We don't have to be Jewish mamas to hope and pray that our little ones will grow up to marry godly spouses and establish godly homes, but we can relate to those Jewish mamas, can't we? Joseph was, no doubt, somewhat older than his betrothed, as Mary was probably a young teenager when the angel Gabriel appeared to her. But I wouldn't be surprised to discover that Joseph's Jewish mama had prayed that her son would one day grow up and marry "a nice Jewish girl." And so he did. In fact, Jewish girls—or any other girls—probably didn't come any nicer, or more pure or chaste or humble, than Mary of Nazareth. And so, I'm sure, both Mary's and Joseph's families rejoiced when the couple became engaged.

Now, an engagement in those days was much more formal and binding than they are in today's fickle, commitment-challenged society. Engagements, or betrothals, normally lasted one year, and they were seldom broken. In the rare instance when a betrothal was terminated, it was serious business and could only be instigated by the prospective husband. Women could not end an engagement, nor could they file for divorce after the marriage was consummated. Once they agreed to the union, they had no more say in the matter.

Women, in fact, had little say in many matters of the day, but they were held to a very high accounting when it came to moral purity. The price for falling short of that standard could result in death by stoning. Adultery would certainly fall into that moral failure category.

When the angel Gabriel appeared to Mary in Luke 1:26–38, the young woman's first recorded reaction is that she was *"troubled at his [the angel's] saying, and considered what manner of greeting this was"* (Luke 1:29). What was it about the angel's saying that troubled Mary? The angel had greeted her with the words, *"Rejoice, highly favored one, the Lord is with you; blessed are you among women!"* (Luke 1:28). Mary wasn't necessarily shocked to see an angel, as she had been raised in the strict interpretation of the Hebrew Scriptures, which included a belief in angels and demons. What shocked her was the fact that such a being would not only come to Earth to visit her but would also address her as *"highly favored one"* and *"blessed...among women."*

Mary had a humble heart. That quality, more than anything else, made her a candidate for this awesome honor. She didn't respond to the angel's announcement with pride at having been chosen, but rather with a humility that recognized her own shortcomings and disqualifications for such a privilege. Yet, as we see in the next verses, in addition to a humble heart, Mary had a steadfast faith—not in herself, but in the God of Israel. Even when the angel went on to say in verse 31, *"You will conceive in your womb and bring forth a Son, and shall call His name Jesus,"* she didn't doubt God. She simply asked out of curiosity, *"How can this be, since I do not know a man?"* (Luke 1:34).

Mary was using the word *know* in the biblical sense, meaning she had not been sexually intimate with any man; she was a virgin. Her question as to how this word from the Lord would be accomplished was therefore a logical one, and the angel did not rebuke her for it. Instead he answered her this way:

> *"The Holy Spirit will come upon you, and the power of the Highest will overshadow you; therefore, also, that Holy One who is to be born will be called the Son of God.... For with God nothing will be impossible."*
> —Luke 1: 35, 37

That answer satisfied Mary's curiosity, and even though it meant submitting herself to a lot of problems and inconveniences, including a possible death sentence, she responded with the powerful declaration of faith found in verse 38, *"Behold the maidservant of the Lord! Let it be to me according to your word."*

Having accomplished his heavenly mission, Gabriel departed, leaving Mary to fulfill hers.

The first hurdle for Mary was to tell her beloved Joseph the news, which she obviously did because Matthew 1:19 makes it clear that Joseph was by then aware of Mary's condition. The verse clearly tells us that *"Joseph her husband, being a just man, and not wanting to make her a public example, was minded to put her away secretly."* Now, even though the verse refers to Joseph as Mary's legal husband, they had not yet consummated their marriage. According to Jewish custom, they were still in the betrothal stage of their relationship, but the permanence of the commitment was as sure as if the final vows had been recited. For that reason, Joseph was already referred to as Mary's "husband." As surely as if they had already consummated their union and were living together under the same roof, Joseph had the right to expect Mary to be faithful to him—and to demand justice if she was not.

> *What a painful scenario this must have been! Joseph had been so sure [she] was a chaste virgin.*

Since Joseph knew he had not been with Mary intimately, then the only natural assumption was to conclude that someone else had.

What a painful scenario that must have been! This young woman, whom Joseph had been so sure was a chaste virgin, had seemingly betrayed him with another man. His heart was broken, and Mary's must have been, too, as she tried to convince the man she loved that though she was pregnant, she had not been unfaithful to him.

Evidently, Joseph did not immediately believe Mary's incredible explanation, and he knew he couldn't go through with the marriage. Though he was crushed at what he perceived as Mary's infidelity and deception, he couldn't bring himself to drag her before the religious authorities and risk having her put to death by stoning. Instead, Matthew 1:19 tells us that Joseph, *"being a just man, and not wanting to make her a public example, was minded to put her away secretly."* Joseph was a man of justice and high morals and couldn't overlook what Mary had done, but he was also a man of compassion and tenderness who didn't want to expose her sin and bring on her what could very possibly end up being a death sentence. So he looked for a way to *"put her away secretly."*

That's when God stepped in and sent an angel to appear to Joseph in a dream and to assure him that what Mary had told him regarding the conception of the baby inside her was true.

*"Joseph, son of David, do not be afraid to take to you Mary your wife, for that which is conceived in her is of the Holy Spirit. And she will bring forth a Son, and you shall call His name Jesus, for He will save His people from their sins."*
—Matthew 1:20–21

Not only did the angel tell Joseph to go ahead with his wedding plans because Mary had not been unfaithful, but he also told him that the baby growing inside Mary's womb had been conceived by the Holy Spirit and His name was to be Jesus, or *Yeshua*, meaning "salvation from the Lord." It was important that Joseph knew the name God had chosen for His only Son because Joseph, who would serve as earthly functional father to Jesus, would, according to the custom of the day, be the one to name the Child after He was born.

The stage was set. The Scriptures don't give us much in the way of specific details as to how the community reacted to Mary's pregnancy, but undoubtedly some of them looked askance at both Mary and Joseph, naturally assuming the two had conceived the baby prior to the accepted time of consummating their marriage. However, by Joseph's going ahead with the marriage, Mary's life and that of her most precious Baby were spared.

## A DEVOTED JEWISH MOTHER

One of the best known and most beloved of all Scripture passages is found in Luke 1, following the angel Gabriel's visit to Mary, when this young Jewish girl leaves Nazareth and goes to the hill country, to a city of Judah, to see her older cousin Elizabeth and Elizabeth's husband, Zacharias. Part of the pronouncement the angel had made to Mary included the news that her formerly barren cousin Elizabeth was now pregnant, which may very well have been the reason Mary went *"with haste"*

*The home of Zacharias and Elizabeth may have served as a haven.*

(see Luke 1:39) to see her cousin. The reason may also have been at least partially due to the very fact that she and Joseph knew the community was not going to react well to Mary's pregnancy, and the home of Zacharias and Elizabeth may have served as a haven for Mary during that time.

Whatever the reason, it was upon Mary's arrival at her cousin's home that the passage of Scripture immediately preceding what is commonly known as the Magnificat was uttered. When Elizabeth heard Mary's greeting, her response to her young visitor was:

> *"Blessed are you among women, and blessed is the fruit of your womb! But why is this granted to me, that the mother of my Lord should come to me? For indeed, as soon as the voice of your greeting sounded in my ears, the babe leaped in my womb for joy. Blessed is she who believed, for there will be a fulfillment of those things which were told her from the Lord."*
> —Luke 1:42–45

When Elizabeth heard Mary's voice, the baby within Elizabeth's womb—later to be known as John the Baptist—leaped for joy, apparently recognizing that he had just heard the voice of the woman who was pregnant with the long-awaited promised One, the Messiah. That was enough to convince Elizabeth of the identity of Mary's coming child, and she immediately referred to both Mary and the *"fruit of [her] womb"* as *"blessed."* And then Mary uttered these famous words:

> *"My soul magnifies the Lord, and my spirit has rejoiced in God my Savior. For He has regarded the lowly state of His maidservant; for behold, henceforth all generations will call me blessed. For He who is mighty has done great things for me, and holy is His name. And His mercy is on those who fear Him from generation to generation. He has shown strength with His arm; He has scattered the proud in the imagination of their hearts. He has put down the mighty from their thrones, and exalted the lowly. He*

*has filled the hungry with good things, and the rich He
has sent away empty. He has helped His servant Israel, in
remembrance of His mercy, as He spoke to our fathers, to
Abraham and to his seed forever."*
—Luke 1:46–55

Again, the words of the Magnificat, uttered by this chaste young
virgin, reflect the humility and faith that can come only through
a life submitted to God. Like every woman who awaits the birth
of a child, she no doubt wondered what the future would bring,
particularly since this was so obviously no ordinary child, but
rather the long-awaited Messiah of Israel. How much of that she
understood at that time we can only speculate, though it's almost
certain she would have been familiar enough with the Scriptures
to realize she was indeed the woman chosen of God to bear the
Messiah. What joy there must have been in that anticipation! And
yet...did she even suspect what heartache and suffering would
accompany that joy?

Without doubt there were hardships accompanying this unique
pregnancy and birth, even from the beginning. In addition to the
community's reaction to what seemed a premature physical union
between Joseph and Mary, this very special couple had to contend
with the difficulties of a long journey right at the time when Mary
was ready to deliver her baby. Luke 2 tells the story this way:

*And it came to pass in those days that a decree went
out from Caesar Augustus that all the world should be
registered. This census first took place while Quirinius was
governing Syria. So all went to be registered, everyone to
his own city. Joseph also went up from Galilee, out of the
city of Nazareth, into Judea, to the city of David, which is
called Bethlehem, because he was of the house and lineage
of David, to be registered with Mary, his betrothed wife,
who was with child. So it was, that while they were there,
the days were completed for her to be delivered.*
—Luke 2:1–6

This was no easy journey under the best of conditions, and certainly not in the last stages of pregnancy. Yet they went, possibly arriving at the same time as Mary's first labor pains.

For those of us who have given birth to children, we know that is not a time a pregnant woman wants to be on the road somewhere, or stuck in a town far from home where we know no one, and all the hospitals and motels and inns are full. However, that's the situation in which Joseph and Mary found themselves. Finally, with the contractions increasing and the options for finding shelter quickly running out, this desperate couple took the offer of a bed of hay in a crowded, smelly stable full of animals. And there Mary *"brought forth her firstborn Son"* (Luke 2:7), the Savior of the world.

Though it's been many years since my children were born, I remember how much I appreciated every comfort offered me during and immediately following the birthing process. Mary had none of these comforts. She *did* have a husband who had risked his own reputation to obey God and to protect Mary and her Baby; she also held the promise of God that Jesus would be called *"the Son of the Highest; and the Lord God will give Him the throne of His father David. And He will reign over the house of Jacob forever, and of His kingdom there will be no end"* (Luke 1:32–33). She knew that though her Son's beginnings would be poor and humble, His end would be glorious—though she knew little of what would happen in the interim.

> She knew that her Son's end would be glorious.

Then, of course, there was the visit from the shepherds. These faithful keepers of the flocks had been startled during the night by a birth announcement unparalleled in history.

> *"Do not be afraid, for behold, I bring you good tidings of great joy which will be to all people. For there is born to you this day in the city of David a Savior, who is Christ the Lord. And this will be the sign to you: You will find a Babe wrapped in swaddling cloths, lying in a manger."*
> —Luke 2:10–12

Following this stunning but joyous announcement, the shepherds came quickly to Bethlehem to find the Baby and to verify the heavenly declaration. Once they had done so, they went out to share the good news with anyone who would listen. *"And all those who heard it marveled at those things which were told them by the shepherds"* (Luke 2:18). Mary, on the other hand, *"kept all these things and pondered them in her heart"* (Luke 2:19).

On the eighth day after Jesus's birth, according to Jewish custom and Old Testament law, Joseph and Mary took the Baby to the Temple in Jerusalem to be presented or dedicated to the Lord and to offer the required sacrifices. When Simeon and Anna, two devout Jews who had spent their lives praying and waiting for the promised Messiah, declared Jesus to be the long-awaited One (see Luke 2:21–38), Mary must have tucked away in her heart yet another consideration to ponder in the years to come.

Later, after an approximately two-year stay in Bethlehem, during which the little family received the famous visit from the wise men, and then followed God's directions to hide out in Egypt to avoid Herod's massacre of the innocents, the threesome returned to Nazareth (see Matthew 2:13–15).

The Scriptures shed no further light on the childhood of Jesus, though we do see one instance when Jesus was 12 that tells us quite a bit about His vast knowledge and understanding of the Scriptures, even at that young age. Jesus, along with His family, had come to Jerusalem for one of the prescribed Jewish feasts. There He went to the Temple and became so involved both asking and answering questions of the learned teachers that He missed the last call to join His family's caravan when they left to return home. When Joseph and Mary realized Jesus wasn't with them in the crowd, they became very anxious and returned to Jerusalem to look for Him. There they found Him in the Temple, still discussing the Scriptures with the scribes and teachers, astonishing these learned men with His knowledge.

His parents, however, were not impressed. *"Son,"* Mary asked Him, *"why have You done this to us? Look, Your father and I have sought You anxiously"* (Luke 2:48).

Jesus replied, *"Why did you seek Me? Did you not know that I must be about My Father's business?"* (Luke 2:49). This was not a statement of disrespect, but rather of fact, which His parents, according to verse 50, did not understand. But Mary *"kept all these things in her heart"* (Luke 2:51), as she had so many other words and events that related to her Son.

Verse 51 also tells us that Jesus went home with them and was *"subject to them,"* while verse 52 makes the final statement about Jesus before He became an adult: *"And Jesus increased in wisdom and stature, and in favor with God and men."*

## A FAITHFUL JEWISH BELIEVER

Mary of Nazareth went from being a nice Jewish girl to being a devoted Jewish mother and, finally, a faithful Jewish believer. Of course, she had always been a faithful Jewish believer in that she followed the Old Testament laws and customs as best she could, and trusted and believed in the God of Israel, even to the point of submitting to His word regarding the bearing of His Son on Earth. But it took longer for her to fully comprehend exactly who this Son of hers truly was.

*That relationship changed drastically when Jesus was about 30 years old.*

Yes, Mary knew of His unique conception and the many promises for His life, but she was also a mother who carried her Baby in her womb, bore Him in a stable, and raised Him in the fear and admonition of the Lord. She loved Jesus as any mother would love her son, and there must have been times when it was very difficult to separate what she knew had been promised about and through Him from the everyday existence of a mother-son relationship.

That relationship changed drastically when Jesus was about 30 years old, not long after Jesus's baptism by John. Now most scholars believe Joseph was dead by that time, leaving Mary a widow long before her 50th birthday. During a wedding at Cana, where both Mary and Jesus were among the guests, the host ran out of wine. Mary obviously knew enough about her unique Son's identity that she didn't doubt He could fix the situation, and so she pointed out to Him that the wine had run out, assuming He would somehow provide more (see John 2:1–3).

Jesus's response was the dividing line in their relationship, the statement that moved Him from a place of relating to her strictly as her Son to the place of being her Lord. *"Woman, what does your concern have to do with Me?"* He asked her. *"My hour has not yet come"* (John 2:4).

It was a gentle but firm rebuke, and she took it as such, bowing to His authority when she said to the servants, *"Whatever He says to you, do it"* (John 2:5). Jesus, of course, went on to turn the water into wine, in essence launching His public ministry (see John 2:6–11).

From then on, throughout the three years of that public ministry, we see little of Mary other than the few occasions where she and her other children came to see Jesus in hopes of convincing Him to be a bit less controversial. It seems, however special or divine the call on our children's lives, we mothers want to keep them safe, regardless of the cost. Mary was no different in that respect.

When we finally see Mary again, it is approximately three years later, as she stands with a broken heart—the one in which she stored up so many memories to ponder over the years— watching her beloved Son die a cruel and agonizing death on the Cross. It was at that point that Jesus, though dying as the Savior of the world and still Lord of all— including Mary—momentarily reverted to His position as Mary's Firstborn and commended His mother's care to John, *"the disciple whom He loved,"* who consequently *"took her to his own home"* (see John 19:25–27). It was a precious and unselfish gift of love from a Son to His mother, and a vote of trust and confidence in the young disciple John as well.

And so, with the exception of her appearance at the empty tomb of the risen Jesus, we don't hear of or see Mary again until the first chapter of Acts, when she is gathered with the disciples in the upper room, continuing *"with one accord in prayer and supplication"* (Acts 1:14). Mary, the nice Jewish girl and devoted Jewish mother, was now a faithful Jewish believer, still loving and longing for the Man-child who was her earthly Son but also worshiping the risen Lord He had proven Himself to be.

Mary had come full circle, fulfilling the calling of God on her life, beginning with submitting herself to whatever God had purposed *"according to [His] word"* and ending at that same place. She had been through a lot of joys and heartaches, troubles and triumphs, as all of us endure in our lifetimes. But spiritually, she was right where she needed to be—the place we all need to be, not only to fulfill our own destinies but those of our children as well.

> *"Happy is the son whose faith in his mother remains unchallenged."*
> **—Louisa May Alcott, author**

## Something to Think About/ Enter in Your Journal:

1. Have you ever had the idea that Mary was just too far separated from you—or anyone else in this world, for that matter—for you to be able to relate to her in any way? If so, how has this brief study of her life changed your thinking on that matter?

2. What are some of the thoughts and events about your own children that you've stored away in your heart and pondered over the years?

3. How can Mary's example of humility and faith help you in dealing with child-rearing issues of your own?

*"A mother understands what a child does not say."*
**—Jewish Proverb**

## A MOTHER'S PRAYER:

*Father, thank You for the godly example of Mary of Nazareth. Thank You for her faith and humility, and thank You for choosing her to bring forth Your Son to save us from our sins. Show me, Lord, what You want me to learn from Mary's life and example. In Jesus's name. Amen.*

**"The words of Mary, 'be it unto me as you say,' when the angel tells her that she will become pregnant with a child from the Holy Spirit, inspire me every day to be a better mother, a better woman, and a better Christian. Her words reveal what God knew about Mary, that she had an undivided heart for God. I can see why the Lord chose her, and every time I want the Lord to do something for me or for my children, I must ask myself if I'm willing to graciously accept whatever way the Lord chooses to bring it about."**
**—Marilynn Griffith, author**

# About Kathi Macias

A mother and grandmother, Kathi and her husband, Al, call California home. With women's ministry as one of her primary interests, Kathi is a popular speaker for women's retreats, conferences, and churches.

An award-winning author, Kathi has written more than 20 books, including two of her New Hope Publishers titles, *Beyond Me, Living a You-First Life in a Me-First World* and *How Can I Run a Tight Ship When I'm Surrounded by Loose Cannons?*, *Proverbs 31 Discoveries for Yielding to the Master of the Seas*.

Kathi is also author of the best-selling devotional *A Moment a Day*, and the popular "Matthews" mystery novels. Her most recent novel, *Emma Jean Reborn*, is being put into script form by playwright Barry Scott. She has written commentary for Thomas Nelson's *Spirit-Filled Life Bible* (Student Edition) and was part of the devotional writing team for Zondervan's *New Women's Devotional Bible*. She has ghostwritten for several prominent individuals including Josh McDowell; former NFL player Rosey Grier; and the late chaplain of the United States Senate, Richard Halverson.

Kathi has won many awards, including the Angel Award from Excellence in Media, fiction awards from the San Diego Christian Writers Guild, and the grand prize in an international writing contest.

**What others are saying about Kathi and *Mothers of the Bible Speak to Mothers Today*:**

"The mothers of the Bible have much insight to offer mothers today, and Kathi Macias does an excellent job of sharing the valuable lessons gleaned from their lives. This book will bless any contemporary mom's heart with its practical, relevant guidance and encouragement."—**Dianne Neal Matthews,** author of *The One Year Women of the Bible*

"This book is a great addition to your personal library if you value solid parenting advice. *Mothers of the Bible Speak to Mothers of Today* is a must-read for the mom who wants to please God while teaching her children to pursue Him too."—**Stacy Hawkins Adams**, author of *Watercolored Pearls, Nothing but the Right Thing, and Speak to My Heart*

"A must for all mothers! Through *Mothers of the Bible Speak to Mothers of Today*, you will see another side of our biblical ancestors...one that is down-to-earth and relatable. In her usual style of wit and wisdom, Kathi Macias writes of the blessing and heartache experienced by mothers throughout the ages. You will learn, grow, and mature throughout these pages." —**Jan Coates,** author/speaker/consultant

# Other New Hope Books for Moms

**Coach Mom**
*7 Strategies for Organizing Your Family
into an All-Star Team*
Brenna Stull
ISBN-10: 1-59669-022-4
ISBN-13: 978-1-59669-022-6

**How Can I Run a Tight Ship When
I'm Surrounded by Loose Cannons?**
*Proverbs 31 Discoveries for Yielding to
the Master of the Seas*
Kathi Macias
ISBN-10: 1-59669-204-9
ISBN-13: 978-1-59669-204-6

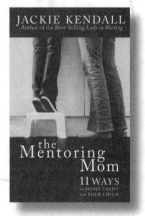

**The Mentoring Mom**
*11 Ways to Model Christ for Your Child*
Jackie Kendall
ISBN-10: 1-59669-005-4
ISBN-13: 978-1-59669-005-9

**Available in bookstores everywhere**

For information about these books or any New Hope product,
visit www.newhopepublishers.com.